THE ULTIMATE

JUICES & SMOOTHIES

ENCYCLOPEDIA

THE ULTIMATE
JUICES &
SMOOTHIES
ENCYCLOPEDIA

YOUR ESSENTIAL GUIDE TO HEALTHY
AND DELICIOUS DRINKS

JILL HAMILTON

THUNDER BAY
P·R·E·S·S

SAN DIEGO

Thunder Bay Press
An imprint of the Baker & Taylor Publishing Group
10350 Barnes Canyon Road, San Diego, CA 92121
www.thunderbaybooks.com

Moseley Road Inc. www.moseleyroad.com
Publisher: Sean Moore
General Manager: Karen Prince
Editorial Director: Damien Moore
Art Director: Tina Vaughan
Production Director: Adam Moore

Editorial: Jill Hamilton, Serena Dilnot
Design: Philippa Baile and Duncan Youel, www.oiloften.co.uk
Photography: Jeremy Baile, Andrew Ridge, Becca MacPhee,
Luke Harris at RGB Digital Ltd, www.rgbdigital.co.uk

All notations of errors or omissions should be addressed to Thunder Bay
Press, Editorial Department, at the above address. All other correspondence
(author inquiries, permissions) concerning the content of this book should be
addressed to Moseley Road Inc.,123 Main St., Irvington, NY 10533, United
States.

Library of Congress Cataloging-in-Publication Data

The ultimate juices and smoothies encyclopedia / the editors of iDrink.com.
    pages cm
 Includes bibliographical references and index.
 ISBN 978-1-62686-051-3 (alk. paper) -- ISBN 1-62686-051-3 (alk. paper)
1. Smoothies (Beverages)--Encyclopedias. 2. Fruit juices--Encyclopedias. I.
iDrink (Firm)
 TX840.J84U48 2014
 641.6'403--dc23
                                    2013044602

Printed in China.
2 3 4 5 18 17 16 15 14

CONTENTS

JUICES

SMOOTHIES

INTRODUCTION

In recent decades, researchers have developed a solid base of science to back up the mantra that generations of mothers preached to their recalcitrant kids: "eat your greens, they're good for you!" According to the World Health Organization, "unhealthy diets and physical inactivity are key risk factors for the major noncommunicable diseases such as cardiovascular diseases, cancer, and diabetes." Like the overwhelming majority of reputable nutrition experts around the world, the World Health Organization comes to the same conclusion as our mothers and grandmothers: the best way to ward off the twin evils of fast food and sluggish feet is to "increase consumption of fruit and vegetables."

5-A-DAY

The now ubiquitous 5-a-day campaign seen on food packaging, along produce aisles in supermarkets, and in schools everywhere is based on the World Health Organization's recommendation that we should all consume a minimum of 14 oz of fruit and vegetables each day as part of an average, healthy, balanced diet. By improving our diet, we increase our energy levels and are more likely to perform and enjoy physical activity—kicking off a virtuous cycle of ever-improving health and fitness. It's that simple! And that's where juices and smoothies come into the picture. They are healthy, quick

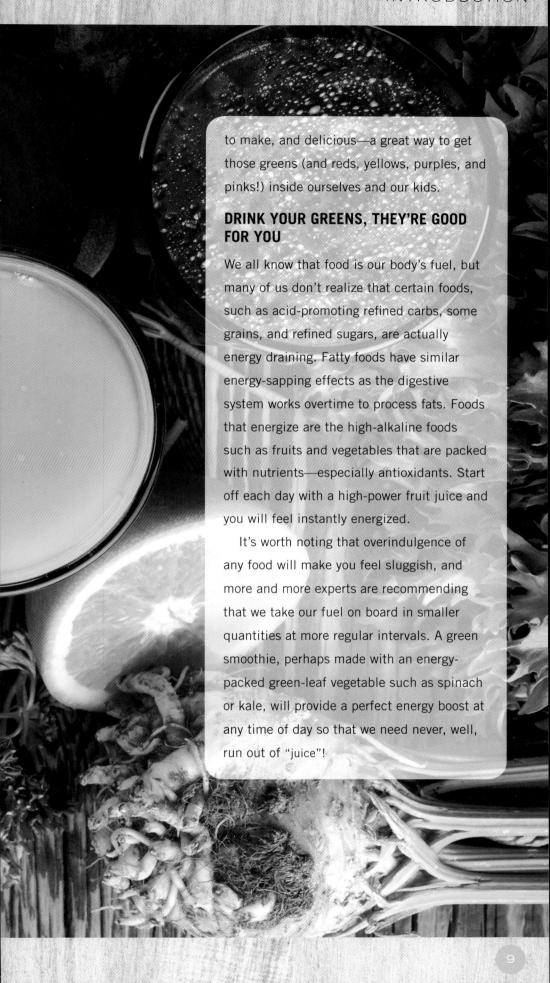

to make, and delicious—a great way to get those greens (and reds, yellows, purples, and pinks!) inside ourselves and our kids.

DRINK YOUR GREENS, THEY'RE GOOD FOR YOU

We all know that food is our body's fuel, but many of us don't realize that certain foods, such as acid-promoting refined carbs, some grains, and refined sugars, are actually energy draining. Fatty foods have similar energy-sapping effects as the digestive system works overtime to process fats. Foods that energize are the high-alkaline foods such as fruits and vegetables that are packed with nutrients—especially antioxidants. Start off each day with a high-power fruit juice and you will feel instantly energized.

It's worth noting that overindulgence of any food will make you feel sluggish, and more and more experts are recommending that we take our fuel on board in smaller quantities at more regular intervals. A green smoothie, perhaps made with an energy-packed green-leaf vegetable such as spinach or kale, will provide a perfect energy boost at any time of day so that we need never, well, run out of "juice"!

FAST FOOD

Juices and smoothies are incredibly easy to make (no recipe should take longer than ten minutes to prepare). The ever-rising tide of health consciousness has led to a raft of super-efficient food processors, blenders, and juicers that make the production of deliciously tempting health drinks easier than ever. Energy-boosting berries—and other fruits and vegetables suitable for juices and smoothies—can be bought frozen from the supermarket, so they can be conveniently stored in the freezer with no need to dilute your ingredients with ice to enjoy a refreshingly chilled health drink every morning.

TASTY TREATS

Juices and smoothies are genuinely delicious as well as nutritious. Fruit juices are naturally sweet so few children need coaxing to enjoy a fruit juice—especially if strawberries or raspberries are involved in the mix. Even the dreaded green vegetables can be made more appetizing when combined with naturally sweet carrot juice. Presented in a sparkling glass with a suitable garnish, juices and smoothies can be quite beautiful to look at too—a far cry from the sorrowful side portion of spinach that kids of previous generations poked around their plates with expressions of loathing. They are fun creations to be positively relished!

FIVE REASONS TO GET FIVE-A-DAY

• Fruit and vegetables contribute to a healthy and balanced diet.

• They're an excellent source of vitamins and minerals, including folate, vitamin C, and potassium.

• They're low in fat and an excellent source of dietary fiber, which helps maintain a healthy gut and prevent digestive problems.

• They can help reduce the risk of heart disease, stroke, and some cancers.

• They taste delicious and there's a huge variety to choose from.

FINISHING TOUCHES

Just like alcoholic cocktails, fruit and vegetable juices and smoothies can be decorated with subtle or not-so-subtle embellishments that add to the sense of occasion when presented to your dinner guests (or even just to brighten your family breakfast). Slices of citrus fruit such as lemon or lime can be wedged onto the edge of the glass (as can cucumber on a veggie juice); olives, grapes, or cherry tomatoes can be impaled on cocktail sticks; whole berries or fruit segments can be dropped into a transparent juice or floated on top of a creamy smoothie; and sprigs of mint, parsley, or other herbs can add texture and color. And why stop there? Straws, umbrellas, and even sparklers can all add to the fun.

Flip through the pages of this book and select a recipe that appeals to you, whether to quench your thirst, boost your energy, improve your health, or indulge your taste buds. And don't feel you need to stick rigidly to a recipe—improvisation and experimentation is a major part of the fun of juicing. Good health!

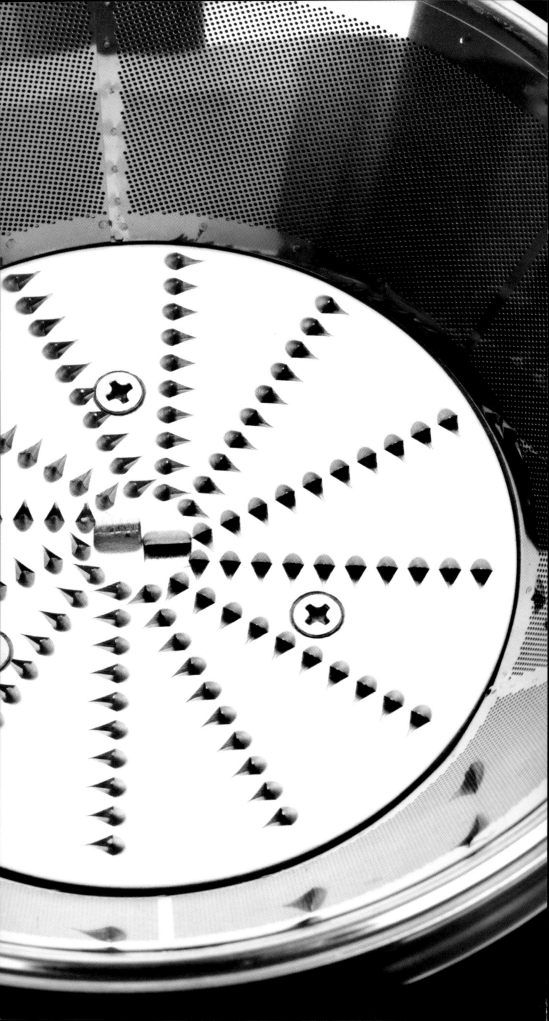

WHY MAKE
JUICES
AND SMOOTHIES?

WHY? BECAUSE IT'S THE EASIEST WAY TO ENSURE THAT YOU AND YOUR ENTIRE FAMILY CONSUME THE RECOMMENDED DAILY ALLOWANCE OF VEGETABLES AND FRUITS—A WHOPPING FIVE ORDERS A DAY, WHICH CAN BE DIFFICULT IF YOU CAN'T TALK YOUR CHILD INTO A SINGLE CARROT. AND, FOR ADULTS, JUICES AND SMOOTHIES ARE THE BEST AND MOST NUTRITIOUS WAY TO CLEANSE AND DETOXIFY THE BODY OR TO GO ON A DIET. SO SET UP YOUR EQUIPMENT AND GET A SELECTION OF FRUITS AND VEGETABLES. WELCOME TO THE WORLD OF RAW FOODS!

WHY JUICE?

For those who are happy to munch on an apple or a carrot to extract a host of vital nutrients direct from the raw material all's well and good, but for those of us who can't get excited about fruits and veges, juices are a lifesaver—much of the goodness of the fruit is magically converted into an appetizing and easily digestible juice that can be enjoyed at breakfast, or as an energy-boosting treat at any time of day.

FUN FOR KIDS!

For kids especially, the process of creating a juice from scratch is fascinating in itself and they love to watch as the often-uninspiring raw material is transformed in a matter of seconds into a sparkling, silky-smooth or crystal clear drink that tastes every bit as good as it looks.

It is worth noting, of course, that juices are often so delicious because the super-efficient modern juicer lives up to its name and removes all the bitter pith and pips leaving only the sweet, sugar-rich juice. Juices are a great way to get a healthy dose of vitamin C and other vital vitamins and minerals into your kids, but they should be enjoyed in moderation. The dietary fiber and other goodness that is lost in the juicing process will have to be replaced elsewhere in your child's diet.

HOMEMADE HEALTH

Having said that, it is much better to provide your children with homemade juice from locally grown, organic produce than to offer them many of the off-the-shelf juices that usually contain added sugar and are relatively low in nutrient value. This is especially true in the case of some popular carbonated drinks and "juices," which actually may contain very little fruit juice at all. With homemade juices you know that the fruit is fresh and nutritious, and by selecting organic fruit you can avoid residue from the pesticides that are used in many intensive farming methods.

FREEZING FRUIT

When you do buy (or pick) a fine crop of fresh fruits, conserve surplus fruit by peeling and chopping as you would in preparation for the juicer and immediately store the fruit segments in plastic bags in your freezer for use at a later date. Fruit added to the juicer straight from the freezer is far preferable to fruit that has been left lying around for a few days losing its goodness. Frozen fruit retains most of the nutrients and there's no need to dilute and chill the drink with additional ice. It emerges deliciously chilled straight from the juicer.

WHY SMOOTHIES?

Smoothies are made in a simple blender rather than with a specialist juicer—in many cases the fruit or vegetable can simply be washed, chopped up, and dropped into the blender, retaining all the goodness of the raw material. Sometimes, however, a little more preparation is required as peel, stones, and cores have to be removed before blending begins.

PACKED WITH GOODNESS

The health benefits of smoothies are substantial. Certain fruits and vegetables contain vital nutrients that are particularly recommended for preventing common illnesses and maintaining the health of the cardiovascular system, cleansing the digestive system, or promoting the growth of healthy bones. Their vitamins help enzymes in your body process food into energy, maintain your body's hormonal balance, and protect the immune system. Meanwhile, the many vital minerals found in fruit and vegetables—such as calcium, iron, and magnesium—help protect the nervous system and build strong muscles, bones, teeth, and hair. Fruits also contain powerful antioxidants that combat the effects of aging and protect the body against chronic illnesses. This book contains a whole host of recipes designed for their targeted health benefits.

INDULGENT DELIGHTS

Pure-fruit smoothies and pure-vegetable, or "green," smoothies are usually high in dietary fiber and are generally more wholesome than juices from which the "pulp" is extracted and discarded. Generally speaking, smoothies can and should be enjoyed more frequently than juices. However, as well as being a nutrient-packed health drink, smoothies, as their name suggests, can be a sumptuous, creamy indulgence. By blending with milk, cream, or ice cream, smoothies can be used to create deliciously tempting (and high-calorie) desserts. Children, especially, find the addition of cocoa or grated chocolate irresistible and such concoctions should be saved as a special treat rather than being served up on a day-to-day basis. For those who enjoy more savory foods, smoothies can also be livened up with herbs and spices, such as ginger or cinnamon. Alcohol can be added to add a bit of sparkle to a dinner-party dessert smoothie. In short, there is a smoothie out there for everyone!

EQUIPMENT

JUICING EQUIPMENT

Juicing is big business nowadays and you only need to take a quick look online to see how easy it might be to part with hundreds of dollars buying a state of the art juicer. However, one of the many refreshing things about juicing is that you can get started with minimal equipment. So what's best for your needs: the humble citrus juicer, a blender, or a juicer? And what's the difference anyway?

THE CITRUS JUICER

The most basic juicer is the citrus press, the humble lemon squeezer that you no doubt have hidden away in a kitchen drawer somewhere along with the egg slicer, ice-cream scoop, and a host of other occasional-use gadgets (some more useful than others). The citrus press has the advantage of being cheap and quick to use, you simply slice the fruit in half (horizontally, across its segments) and press the cut end down onto the "reamer," which is itself a half-lemon shape, grooved to increase the pressure on the fruit flesh and to allow the juice to run down into the bowl. In the classic, usually glass, model, the pith and pips are separated from the juice by a simple circle of nodules surrounding the reamer.
A flat handle is positioned at ninety degrees to a spout. This is still a great option for that refreshing glass of fresh orange juice.

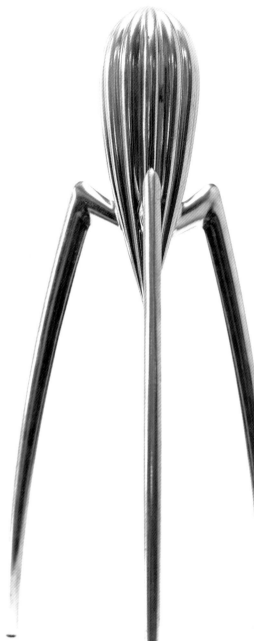

STOP THE PRESS!

In 1990, the citrus juicer emerged from the dark recesses of the kitchen-clutter cabinet and stepped into the limelight (pun intended!) as the now iconic Juicy Salif lemon squeezer. Like a scale model of something from H.G. Wells' sci-fi novel *War of the Worlds*, it is the creation of the design whizz Philippe Starck. Standing at just under a foot tall, the reamer is suspended on three spidery legs and a glass is placed underneath to collect the juice (most of the time). Like much of Starck's work, it is somewhat controversial and is as much a work of art and a dinner-party talking point as a practical kitchen implement. Starck's juicer can be seen in New York's Museum of Modern Art or in trendy kitchens everywhere—available in aluminum or gold plate!

Starck has imbued what was a perfectly adequate kitchen-drawer filler with aspirational desirability, indications of intellectual meaning, and a mythical lack of juicing prowess.

MICHAEL CZERWINKSKI *(LONDON DESIGN MUSEUM)*

BLENDERS

Another relatively simple and efficient option is to use a handheld blender. They are small and convenient, easy to store, and easy to clean (check that the shaft that houses the blade can be detached from the handle and that it is dishwasher safe). It is also worth paying a little more for a handheld blender that is powerful enough to crush ice and berries taken straight from the freezer. A word of warning, the time you save cleaning the handheld blender will seem less of an advantage when you find yourself running late for the office because you spent twenty minutes cleaning tomato juice off the kitchen worktop and wall, and had to change the pristine white shirt you had ironed especially the night before! Make sure you blend the ingredients in a suitable splash-proof container—before you dress for the office. Or, consider investing in a more substantial blender with a large glass or plastic pitcher with a wide, metal base for stability, and a lid! You should still be looking for a machine with a minimum 400 watts of power and ice-crushing capability.

JUICING ACCESSORIES

Many of the accessories you need for juicing will already be in your kitchen, such as scales to weigh solid ingredients and a measuring cup to ensure that you have the correct proportions of liquid ingredients for each recipe. A vegetable peeler is needed to remove the skin from certain foods—especially many non-organic fruits and root vegetables. A small, sharp fruit knife and a larger chopping blade are a must, along with a suitable chopping board. Graters, too, are useful for citrus zest or spices such as nutmeg. A long handled spoon or swizzle stick will be ideal for combining juices (and the spoon can help you retrieve the maximum amount of those thicker smoothies that tend to stick stubbornly to the bottom of the jug). Of course, a range of glasses will be needed to display your wonderful creations to their best advantage. Finally, when you really start taking your juicing seriously, you might want add a few luxury items, such as an apple or pineapple corer.

THE WHOLE JUICE, AND NOTHING BUT THE JUICE.

The key difference between blenders and juicers is simply that blenders don't separate the juice from the pulp. If you prefer your health drinks super smooth and easily digestible, with no hint of pith or pip, then you need to consider a juicer, which will separate the juice from the fibers of fruit and vegetables. Prices range from inexpensive to exorbitant but, as in all things in life, you generally get what you pay for.

There are two different types of juicers: centrifugal and masticating. Centrifugal juicers have a perforated metal basket usually complete with minute "teeth" that grind the fruit or veg as the basket spins. The centrifugal force pushes the liquid through the perforations to separate the juice from the pulp. Masticating juicers are more substantial (and considerably more expensive) machines that use a powerful screwlike mechanism to pulverize the food into mush, which is forced down a tapered tube and through a wire mesh so that the juice is separated from the pulp. They extract larger amounts of juice than centrifugal models and therefore larger quantities of nutrients, and it is argued that their slowly rotating cutters do not expose the juice to oxidization so that it maintains its nutritional value for longer and doesn't have to be drunk immediately. The quality of a masticating juicer is best gauged by the quantity and dryness of the pulp that is left behind after the juicing process; cheaper

juicers leave a higher quantity of damp "mush," whereas a hi-end machine will leave remarkably little pulp that is bone dry.

WHEATGRASS JUICERS

Leafy vegetables and wheatgrass are packed with nutrition but their "stringiness" means they can only be juiced in specialized juicers—centrifugal juicers simply cannot process them. Some of the hi-end masticating juicers can cope with such greens or have special wheatgrass attachments to do the job, but such machines are often expensive or bulky. Fortunately, there are specialized expeller press juicers that are relatively cheap and easy to use. Many models are manually operated with a crank handle and attach to a tabletop using a simple vice to provide stability without bulk. Since they're light and don't require electricity, you can take your wheatgrass juicer with you on your travels and need never do without your favorite green drinks. In fact, since such "specialized" machines juice a variety of fruit and vegetables other than wheatgrass, this may be the only juicer you need.

Whichever machine best suits your needs and your budget, check that it dismantles easily so that it can be cleaned quickly and thoroughly. Nothing is more likely to turn you off juicing than the thought of laboriously scrubbing to clean gunk from the contraption every time you make a drink.

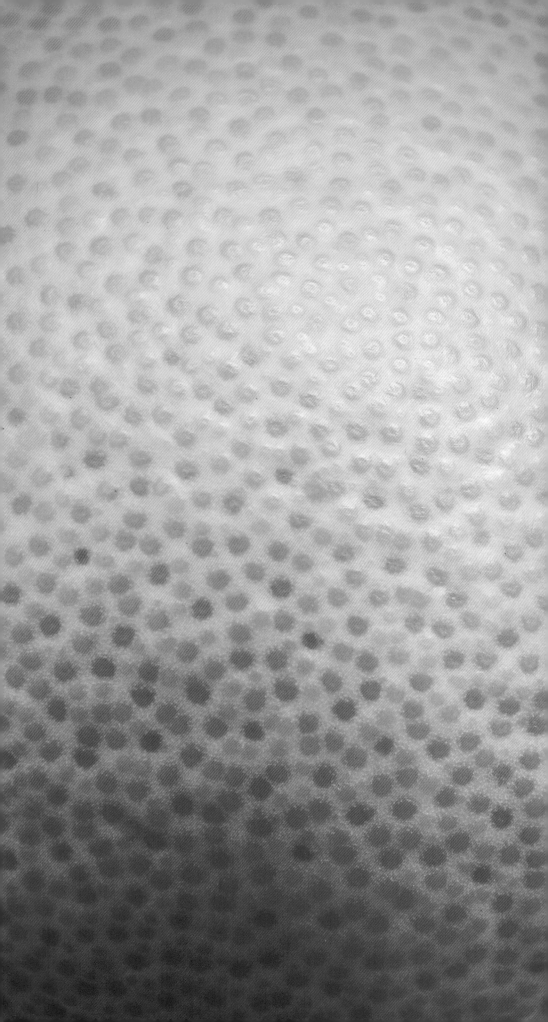

NUTRITIONAL
BENEFITS

VISUAL GLOSSARY

LET'S TAKE SOME TIME TO GET TO KNOW THE
STARS OF THE SHOW: THE INDIVIDUAL FRUITS AND
VEGETABLES THAT APPEAR IN SO MANY WONDERFUL
JUICES AND SMOOTHIES. EACH HAS ITS OWN VARIETY
OF NUTRITIONAL BENEFITS, AND LEARNING A LITTLE
ABOUT THOSE NUTRIENTS CAN GO A LONG WAY TO
HELPING YOU CREATE A HEALTHY BALANCED DIET FOR
YOU AND YOUR FAMILY.

APPLES

There are over 7,500 varieties of apple out there, and some are particularly good for juicing, including the ubiquitous Cox's Orange Pippin and the Golden Russet. As a rule of thumb, the greener an apple's skin, the sharper its juice will taste, so if you enjoy a tart flavor, opt for Granny Smith or McIntosh apples. Whichever variety you choose, select fresh fruit with firm undamaged skin. Avoid those with waxy skins, as this often disguises a woolly, flavorless fruit. Apples should be washed thoroughly and chopped into quarters. They do not necessarily need to be peeled or cored—apple seeds are a valuable source of potassium. Apples are also full of a fiber called pectin, which is classed as a soluble, fermentable, and viscous fiber, a combination that gives it a huge list of health benefits. They are also high in antioxidants— compounds that help repair oxidation damage that occurs during normal cell activity.

BEST FOR
Pectin and vitamin C, which lower cholesterol.

CALORIES
52/3.5 oz

PREPARATION
Wash and chop into quarters. No need to peel or core.

Freshly squeezed apple juice

A variety of different apples

APRICOTS

Hailing from the peach family, apricots are firm, attractive, pinky-orange fruits with velvety skin and a distinctive bittersweet flavor that is something between a peach and a plum. Widely recognized as a superfood, they are a good source of fiber and beta-carotene and an excellent source of vitamin A, which is vital for healthy eyesight and a leading agent in the battle against age-related macular degeneration—the primary cause of vision loss in older adults. Known to the Greeks as "golden eggs of the sun," apricots are also high in vitamin C and minerals such as calcium and magnesium. They are wonderful antioxidant cleansers and are often recommended for respiratory problems. However, they are not one of the juiciest fruits, so you will need several to produce a reasonable quantity of juice and they are best mixed with another juice, or diluted with water. Although the stone is edible it should be removed before juicing.

Freshly cut apricots

BEST FOR
Vitamin A/beta-carotene, to promote healthy eyes, skin, hair, and bones.

CALORIES
48/3.5 oz

PREPARATION
Wash, remove stone. No need to peel.

AVOCADOS

Like apricots and bananas, avocados are not great for juicing. Plus, they tend to receive a lot of bad press for their high fat content and high calorie count. Nevertheless, they are packed with goodness and can be successfully blended with other juicier fruits and vegetables. They are high in vitamin E, which boosts the immune system, and their cholesterol-lowering properties, along with their folate content, help keep your heart healthy. Folate (the natural form of folic acid) helps the body produce red blood cells and has several other vital functions. It is particularly important for pregnant women because it reduces the risk of birth defects. Avocados are also an excellent source of potassium, which many health experts claim provides protection against premature aging. As well as improving your complexion, potassium helps combat fatigue and lethargy.

Freshly cut avocado

BEST FOR
Folate, to produce healthy red blood cells.

CALORIES
160/3.5 oz

PREPARATION
Wash, cut in half to remove stone, scoop flesh into blender.

BANANAS

For juicing, use soft bananas, chopped up or mashed and combined with a juicier fruit that will flush the banana through the juicer. Bananas come into their own in smoothies as they can be blended more successfully and provide a great flavor along with a lovely creamy texture. Bananas are rich in potassium, a mineral vital to the functioning of body cells, and vitamin B6, which metabolizes proteins, sugars, and fatty acids. They are a good source of manganese and magnesium—essential trace minerals involved in the production of cartilage as well as being required for healthy bones and for normal nerve function. Bananas also promote the release of serotonin, the body's natural "happy" chemical that is often prescribed in drug form as an antidepressant. The banana has been described as "a sleeping pill in a peel"—in addition to the soothing serotonin, the magnesium acts as a muscle relaxant.

BEST FOR
Vitamin B6 (pyridoxine), which preserves nerves and skin.

CALORIES
79/3.5 oz

PREPARATION
Peel and chop into segments.

Freshly cut organic banana

Banana smoothie

BLACKBERRIES

Blackberries grow on thorny brambles that can make picking them in the wild a challenging yet highly rewarding adventure. Once ripe (but not overly so), they produce an ideal mixing juice that is rich in nutrients. They are high in dietary fiber, which aids digestion and improves cardiovascular health. As a bonus, fiber helps you to feel satisfied longer, which makes this low-calorie fruit a great diet food. Blackberries are also rich in antioxidants. They have anthocyanins, which help prevent the effects of aging, and are thought to help combat cancer and neurological diseases. Gallic acid in blackberries is an antioxidant used to help treat psoriasis and hemorrhoids. Blackberries are also a good source of vitamins A and C, which work together as antioxidants to help strengthen the immune system. Blackberries do not stay fresh for long so use immediately or store them in the freezer for later use.

BEST FOR
Vitamin C for healthy skin, blood, and bones.

CALORIES
43/3.5 oz

PREPARATION
Wash and use immediately.

Fresh blackberry juice

BLACKCURRANTS

Fresh currants are dark purple, almost black, with a glossy skin and a delightfully tangy taste. These juicy and acidic berries are fabulously rich in vitamin C and iron. Iron is an essential mineral whose main function is to help distribute oxygen from the lungs. When iron is low, oxygen circulates more slowly, often resulting in fatigue, irritability, and headaches. Significant deficiency can lead to anemia. Women are more likely to develop iron deficiency, partly because of the loss of red blood cells during menstruation. Adolescents, both male and female, may also be lacking, due to their rapid growth. Furthermore, iron absorption can be impaired by the frequent drinking of tea and coffee, so replace at least one of your daily caffeine boosters with another drink—say, a delicious blackcurrant juice. If not used immediately, store currants in the refrigerator where they will keep fresh for several days.

Bowl of freshly picked blackcurrants

BEST FOR
Vitamin C/iron to metabolize proteins and promote growth.

CALORIES
63/3.5 oz

PREPARATION
Wash and use immediately.

BLUEBERRIES

Blueberries have been enjoyed by Native Americans for centuries, and are one of the few fruits that originated in North America. Commonly hailed as the ultimate superfood, blueberries are now hugely popular all around the world and are famed for having one of the highest antioxidant capacities among all fruits and vegetables. Blueberries are very rich in vitamin K, which has several important functions, including helping wounds heal properly and building strong bones. Otherwise, blueberries are thought to be beneficial for everything from promoting a healthy urinary tract to reducing belly fat, preserving eyesight, and combatting heart disease. Recent studies suggest that blueberries may also help improve memory and slow down or postpone the onset of other cognitive problems associated with aging. The anthocyanin, selenium, and a host of other vitamins and minerals abundant in blueberries may prevent and ease the symptoms of neurotic disorders and promote the health of the central nervous system. Sadly, they don't keep well after harvesting, but they can be frozen for later use.

BEST FOR
Antioxidants, for a healthy immune system.

CALORIES
57/3.5 oz

PREPARATION
Wash and use immediately.

Blueberry smoothie

CHERRIES

Although rather fiddly to prepare, this delicious red fruit has so many health-boosting benefits that it's well worth the effort. Cherries are one of the few known food sources of melatonin, a naturally occurring hormone that helps to regulate the body's sleep patterns. They are also a fantastic source of vitamin C and vitamin A. Anthocyanins in cherries have a marked anti-inflammatory action and are highly effective in treating gout. These fabulous little fruits also contain quercetin, which is said to prevent damaging lesions—thought to be a predictor of cancerous tumors—from forming in the colon. As if all of this wasn't enough, cherries are low in sugar compared to most other fruits, which makes them an ideal choice for people who want to lose weight.

BEST FOR
Vitamin A (retinol) for healthy eyes, hair, teeth, and skin.

CALORIES
50/3.5 oz

PREPARATION
Wash, cut in half to remove stone. No need to peel.

Bowl of freshly picked cherries

CRANBERRIES

A fruit native to the Americas, and cousin to the similarly super blueberries, these glossy, scarlet berries produce a tart juice that mixes especially well with orange or apple. While familiar nutrients like vitamin C, the important mineral manganese, and fiber play a very important role in cranberries' health benefits, it's actually their amazing cocktail of phytonutrients that makes them stand out from the crowd. Cranberries have been associated with promotion of a healthy urinary tract, and recent tests indicate that they may similarly protect the stomach lining. Other health benefits attributed to cranberries include anti-inflammatory and anti-cancer properties. The latter are now thought to extend to cancers of the breast, colon, lung, and prostate. Choose fresh, plump, bright red fruit, which will keep for several weeks in the refrigerator.

BEST FOR
Manganese to neutralize free radicals and maintain healthy nerves.

CALORIES
46/3.5 oz

PREPARATION
Wash. No need to peel.

GRAPEFRUIT

The grapefruit's Latin name, *Citrus paradisi*, reflects its origins on the paradise island of Barbados in the 18th century, where the fruit grew wild and hung from the trees in clusters like overgrown grapes. Whether or not the fruit is "a taste of paradise" is open to debate—it is way too tangy for some palates. There is no doubt, however, that grapefruit is an excellent source of vitamin C and red varieties are so rich in vitamin A that they are ranked among those fruits with the highest antioxidant activity. Recent studies also suggest that grapefruits may be particularly effective in combatting lung and colon cancers and can significantly lower cholesterol. Again, although both red and yellow grapefruits positively influence cholesterol levels, it is worth noting that red grapefruit is more than twice as effective. So, if you're already healthy and want to stay that way, grapefruits are indeed a heavenly fruit. The controversy arises because certain compounds in grapefruit are known to increase circulating levels of a number of prescription drugs, including statins, and the risk of toxicity associated with such drugs may actually increase when grapefruit is consumed. Therefore, if you're taking any kind of prescription drugs, check with your healthcare practitioner before adding grapefruit juice to your diet.

BEST FOR
Pectin, to improve circulatory or digestive problems.

CALORIES
40/3.5 oz

PREPARATION
Peel and break into segments.

GRAPES

Ideal for juicing, freshly ripened grapes are bursting with goodness, and their health benfits have been appreciated for centuries, if not millennia. Grapes are among the world's oldest and most widely cultivated fruits. Every year the list of health benefits from their consumption grows longer. With their abundance of health-supportive phytonutrients, they benefit the cardiovascular system, respiratory system, immune system, lymphatic system, and nervous system. Another area of special benefit is cancer prevention, especially breast, prostate, and colon cancer. To top it all, resveratrol, a phytonutrient present in grapes, has been shown to increase our chances of aging healthily.

BEST FOR
Resveratrol, to increase longevity.

CALORIES
67/3.5 oz

PREPARATION
Wash, remove stalks. No need to remove pips.

Fresh grape juice

KIWIFRUIT

A furry-skinned berry about the same size as a hen's egg, kiwifruits are often enjoyed by kids in a similar way to a boiled-egg breakfast— slicing off the top and scooping out the delicious emerald flesh with a teaspoon. When juiced, a kiwi produces a thick, green juice that is delicious by itself but is wonderful when mixed with fruits such as pineapple or melon. Positively bursting with vitamin C, they are also an excellent source of magnesium, which offers multiple health benefits that include aiding the transmission of nerve impulses, regulating body temperature, detoxifying the blood, boosting energy production, and promoting the formation of healthy bones and teeth. Magnesium also aids the treatment of migraines, insomnia, and symptoms of depression. It is used to help combat such psychiatric problems as anxiety and panic attacks. Be sure to select firm fruit with unwrinkled skin. Hard fruit can be ripened at room temperature but be sure to store the kiwi away from other fruit— hormones released by them will cause other fruit to ripen too quickly.

BEST FOR
Magnesium, to regulate blood pressure and build strong bones.

CALORIES
61/3.5 oz

PREPARATION
Peel, and chop to fit into feeder tube.

Fresh kiwi juice

LEMONS

Lemons originated in Asia and were brought by the troops of Alexander the Great to Greece where, even then, they were used for medicinal purposes. More recently they were distributed to sailors in the British navy to combat the debilitating effects of scurvy. Today, they are still employed for medicinal purposes in cold remedies, are used in kitchens throughout the world to bring out the flavor of other foods, and are squeezed in water to cleanse the palate (and the fingers!) between meals. They are far too bitter for the average palate and should always be diluted. Remove the skin to avoid contaminating the juice with the wax that is often used to prolong the shelf life of lemons and other fruits. However, preserve as much of the pith as possible as it is rich in flavonoids, which recent studies suggest may have antihistamine, antimicrobial, memory- and even mood-enhancing properties. Although approximately half the size of the average orange, they contain twice the amount of vitamin C.

BEST FOR
Vitamin C, for healthy skin, bones, teeth, and hair.

CALORIES
29/3.5 oz

PREPARATION
Peel, and divide into segments.

Freshly squeezed lemon juice

LIMES

Emerald-green limes are an excellent source of vitamin C and, like lemons, were eaten to prevent the degenerative disease scurvy that was so prevalent among sailors in the 17th and 18th centuries. One of the most important antioxidants in food, vitamin C neutralizes damaging free radicals. Like lemons, limes contain flavonoids that may have anti-cancer properties. They also possess antibiotic properties and have been used in Africa to protect against cholera. The smallest of the citrus fruits, they are also the most perishable so be sure to select an unblemished specimen that feels heavy for its size with a rich green color. Limes can be kept out at room temperature where they will stay fresh for up to one week. Lime juice can be stored for later use. Pour freshly squeezed lime juice in ice cube trays until frozen, then store them in plastic bags in the freezer.

Freshly cut lime

BEST FOR
Vitamin C, for healthy skin, bones, teeth, and hair.

CALORIES
30/3.5 oz

PREPARATION
Peel, and divide into segments.

MANGOS

Often hailed as "the king of fruits," mangos are a delicious tropical superfood with a distinctive fragrance, taste, and texture. Mangos are best to juice when they reach the peak of ripeness and are just starting to give slightly to the touch. Recent research suggests that the polyphenolic antioxidant compounds found in mangos are especially effective in helping to protect against colon, breast, and prostate cancers. Mangos are rich in vitamins and minerals, including vitamin A for healthy skin and vitamin B6 for protecting gray matter. They are an excellent source of vitamin C, potassium, and niacin. Mangos do not last well in the refrigerator and are best left at room temperature where they will keep for three or four days.

BEST FOR
Carotenes, to boost the immune system.

CALORIES
70/3.5 oz

PREPARATION
Slice in half or quarters, remove the stone, and scoop the flesh out of the skin.

MELONS

Yellow melons such as cantaloupe or honeydew varieties produce wonderfully refreshing juice that can be absorbed very quickly by the digestive system, and is great for mixing with a host of other fruits. They are a good source of folic acid, which preserves the nervous system. Watermelons have attracted a good deal of scientific interest in recent years as they have been found to be rich in lycopene—a carotenoid phytonutrient that's especially good for the heart. It's worth noting that lycopene, beta-carotene, and other antioxidants are highest in ripe watermelon—when its flesh is almost red. The seeds in watermelon are a good source of iron, zinc, vitamin E, and essential fatty acids. The rind, too, is full of nutrients but can alter the flavor significantly. You might want to add a little honey if you decide to juice a significant portion of rind.

BEST FOR
Lycopene, for cardiovascular health.

CALORIES
28/3.5 oz

PREPARATION
Slice into quarters, remove the pips if preferred, and cut away the flesh in chunks.

Watermelon juice

Cantaloupe, watermelon, and honeydew

NECTARINES

A close relative of the peach but lacking the velvety skin, nectarines are popular worldwide for their fragrant aroma and unique taste. Like the peach, they originated in China then spread to Central Asia and Europe via the Silk Road. The flesh is juicy and, depending upon the variety, yellow or pale cream in color with a single stone in the center. The seed is very hard and inedible. Nectarines are classified into free-stone variety or clinging variety depending on whether the seed is free or firmly attached to the pulp. As well as being a source of antioxidants, such as vitamin C and vitamin A, nectarines are a good source of some B vitamins, including niacin, pantothenic acid, thiamine, and pyridoxine. They also contain important minerals, including iron, potassium, and phosphorus. Iron is required for red blood cell formation; potassium helps regulate heart rate and blood pressure; and phosphorus helps to preserve the nervous system.

Bowl of nectarines

BEST FOR
Vitamin B3 (niacin), to lower cholesterol.

CALORIES
44/3.5 oz

PREPARATION
Wash, slice to remove the stone. No need to remove skin.

ORANGES

Once regarded as a luxury item available only to the mega-rich, oranges first became more widely available in the 17th century with the establishment of trade routes to India. Commonplace they may be, but they are still a treasure trove in terms of health benefits and their status in the world of juicing, where they provide the base juice for so many wonderful cocktails. Packed with goodness, at the expense of just a few calories, a single orange can provide your full day's quota of vitamin C. It's worth noting that juicing—rather than squeezing—is more beneficial healthwise because it includes the pith that contains the super-antioxidant bioflavonoids that help the body process that precious vitamin C. Note, too, that the seeds are a good source of calcium, magnesium, and potassium, so for the greatest benefit simply peel the orange and juice the flesh, pith, and pips. Aromatic, delicious, and refreshing, fresh orange juice is the classic breakfast drink that provides the perfect start to a day.

BEST FOR
Vitamin C, for healthy bones, teeth, skin, and hair.

CALORIES
46/3.5 oz

PREPARATION
Peel and quarter.

47

PEACHES

Flawless, "peachy" skin is the ideal of most women today, and it is surely not surprising that this beautiful, velvety fruit is found in a host of skincare beauty products. Nor is it surprising that it is full of goodness when sipped as a deliciously refreshing juice or smoothie. Peaches contain health-giving flavonoids that combat free radicals and may play an important role in forestalling many signs of aging and protect against cancer and heart disease. They are a rich source of many vital vitamins and minerals, including vitamin C, vitamin A, potassium, fluoride, copper, and iron. Peaches combine particularly well with pineapple, but are also delicious when mixed with a host of other fruits, including grapes, cherries, and plums. Not for nothing are they called the "nectar of the gods."

BEST FOR
Flavonoids, to delay the aging process.

CALORIES
45/3.5 oz

PREPARATION
Slice in half to remove stone, then chop to feed into juicer.

Freshly picked peaches and juice

PEARS

There are more than 5,000 varieties of pear out there, but they are broadly divided into just two categories: Asian pears, which tend to be firm and crisp (and stay that way); and European pears, which tend to become softer as they ripen, making them ideal for juicing. Although low in calories, pears are packed with the usual suspects in the world of fruity nutrients such as dietary fiber, antioxidants, vitamins, and minerals. Pears are a good source of copper, iron, potassium, and magnesium, as well as vitamin C and a heap of B-complex vitamins. Pears are thought to have a special role to play in the fight against colon cancer, helping to cleanse the colon of carcinogenic toxins. Pears appear in a range of traditional medicines designed to treat such chronic disorders as colitis, arthritis, and gout. Pear juice oxidizes very rapidly, so to obtain the maximum health benefits be sure to drink the juice as soon as it is made.

BEST FOR
Copper, to help your body process iron and protect the nervous system.

CALORIES
60/3.5 oz

PREPARATION
Wash, and chop to fit into juicer.

Freshly squeezed pear juice

PLUMS

Fleshy and succulent, plums are small attractive fruits that originated in China and range in color from yellow to deep purple. They are perhaps most renowned for aiding digestion and helping to relieve constipation, especially in their dried (and often dreaded) form as "prunes." The juicy flesh encases a hard, inedible stone that needs to be removed before juicing. Besides their gentle laxative effect, thanks largely to the presence of sorbitol, plums are a good source of flavonoid polyphenolic antioxidants, which devour the oxygen-derived free radicals that are thought to cause a number of illnesses. They are also a good source of potassium, which helps control the heart rate and blood pressure; vitamin A, which is essential for healthy eyesight; and vitamin K, which is beneficial for bone strength and is thought to help reduce the occurrence of Alzheimer's. Do not peel the fruit, as the skin contains antioxidant pigments and is a good source of fiber.

Ripe plums

BEST FOR
Beta-carotene to boost the immune system.

CALORIES
46/3.5 oz

PREPARATION
Wash, and slice to remove stone. No need to peel.

PINEAPPLE

Perhaps the most distinctive of all fruits, the exotic pineapple originated in the South American tropics and was brought to Europe by Christopher Columbus in 1493. Today, it is hugely popular all around the world and is renowned for its manifold health benefits. It is hailed as being especially good for the digestive system due to the presence of the potent enzyme bromelain, which is anti-inflammatory and considered beneficial in the treatment of acute sinusitis, arthritis, and gout. It is also used to help alleviate chest conditions such as bronchitis and pneumonia. Pineapples are high in thiamine, vitamin B6, and copper, and are an excellent source of vitamin C. They are relatively fiddly to prepare but the nutritional benefits and the distinctive, delightfully refreshing taste are more than worth the effort.

BEST FOR
Bromelain, to aid the digestive system.

CALORIES
50/3.5 oz

PREPARATION
Slice off the crown and base then place the fruit on its base to carefully remove the skin. Cut into chunks to feed into the juicer.

Freshly squeezed pineapple juice

RASPBERRIES

Raspberries are delicately fragrant, pink fruits that, like their cousin the blackberry, grow on sprawling thorny brambles. Like blackberries, they are an aggregate fruit that are actually clusters of many tiny individual fruits, each containing its own seed. The health benefits of raspberries are equally multitudinous and they are credited with strengthening the immune system, protecting against heart disease and liver fibrosis, and promoting wound healing. They are also a good source of the anticarcinogen ellagic acid. All this goodness stems from a plethora of anti-inflammatory and antioxidant phytonutrients and a multitude of minerals, including zinc to help maintain the body's acid/alkaline balance and magnesium, which is vital for a healthy heart. Raspberries are especially rich in manganese, which is important for strong bones. With all these fabulous health benefits, it's great to know that raspberries freeze well and can be enjoyed at any time of the year—and there's no need to defrost them before juicing.

BEST FOR
Vitamin K, which helps prevent postmenopausal bone loss.

CALORIES
53/3.5 oz

PREPARATION
Wash carefully before hulling.

Freshly squeezed raspberry juice

Wild raspberries

STRAWBERRIES

Low in calories but extremely high in vitamin C, strawberries are synonymous with summertime. One of the world's favorite fruits, they are especially popular in milkshakes and smoothies to which they lend their lovely pink color as well as (when fresh from the field at least) lots of wholesome vitamins and minerals. Recent research suggests that strawberries can help maintain healthy blood-sugar levels, and famously promote a healthy heart thanks to their outstanding antioxidant and anti-inflammatory content. A good source of vitamin B, potassium, and magnesium, strawberries make an excellent cleansing juice. But, let's face it, nobody needs an excuse to consume strawberries— their delicious flavor is reason enough. Sadly, strawberries do not keep well but they can be frozen if you cut away the leaves from the base and wash (and dry) them beforehand. Upon thawing, they often become soft or even mushy, but there's no need to defrost them before juicing.

BEST FOR
Iodine, for a healthy thyroid.

CALORIES
33/3.5 oz

PREPARATION
Wash carefully and remove stems.

The strawberry plant

TANGERINES

A number of smaller citrus fruits are orange in color but unrelated to the larger fruit and more intense in flavor, among them, satsumas and tangerines. Tangerines also divide more easily than oranges into 8 to 10 juicy segments. Like oranges, they are low in calories and high in vitamin C, and they are an even more valuable source of antioxidants such as carotenes and vitamin A. Tangerines are a good source of potassium, as well as some important minerals such as copper and magnesium. Like other citrus fruits, they are believed to help protect against a range of cancers, including stomach, mouth, larynx, and pharynx cancers. Some studies indicate benefits for heart disease and strokes, as well as numerous other debilitating conditions such as arthritis, Alzheimer's disease, cataracts, and gallstones. They will store in the refrigerator for a week or so, but enjoy them as early as possible to gain the maximum nutritional benefits.

BEST FOR
Thiamine, to boost the immune system.

CALORIES
53/3.5 oz

PREPARATION
Peel, and divide into segments.

Fresh tangerine juice

BEETS

These modest round root vegetables have recently found unexpected fame as a fashionable superfood. Their unusual rich red color comes from phytochemicals known as betalains, which have an antioxidant and anti-inflammatory role. Beet juice has some effect in lowering blood pressure and increasing blood flow to the brain in older people. Surprisingly, it may also make you run a little bit faster! When used raw, beets are very high in folate, which reduces the risk of fetal defects. The green tops are even more nutritious than the roots, with higher levels of phytonutrients and vitamins C and A, but should not be consumed in large quantities as they contain potentially harmful oxalic acid. The beautiful bright red juice gives a colorful lift to other juices, which dilute its strong taste. Beet juice may turn the urine red; this is not unusual, but can sometimes indicate an underlying problem with iron metabolism. Choose small, firm beets and avoid any with wilting foliage.

BEST FOR
Antioxidants, to help prevent cancer and heart disease.

CALORIES
44/3.5 oz

PREPARATION
Cut off the tops and wash; scrub the roots, cut into quarters and use immediately.

Fresh beet juice

BROCCOLI

Broccoli is blessed with numerous health-enhancing qualities. One of the most powerful superfoods, it is an important source of the detoxifying phytonutrients that are thought to help protect us from cancers of the breast, colon, and prostate. It is also rich in many antioxidant vitamins and minerals, containing more than the daily recommended intake of the vitamins C and K in a single portion, as well as useful amounts of vitamin A, for protecting the health of our eyes and skin, and folate, which is known to reduce fetal abnormalities when taken before conception and during pregnancy. It's a great source of calcium, for maintaining healthy bones, and like many vegetables is very low in calories. The list of broccoli's virtues is almost endless, but sadly it can turn a bit bitter when juiced, so it works best when mixed with sweeter vegetables such as carrots or beets. Choose firm, unbruised dark green heads with no yellowing.

Fresh broccoli juice

BEST FOR
Rich in essential vitamins and minerals for all-round health.

CALORIES
34/3.5 oz

PREPARATION
Rinse and cut into smaller pieces, including the stalk and fresh leaves.

CABBAGE

The smell of overcooked cabbage may have put you off it for life, but think again! It turns out that eating your greens really is a good idea, as the cabbage family is now known to be full of valuable hidden health benefits. Cabbages can be dark green, light green, or red, with red varieties having the highest amount of the beneficial nutrients. When eaten raw, cabbage contains a number of antioxidants, such as polyphenols and glucosinolates, which play an important part in helping to prevent cancer and lower cholesterol. It also has useful amounts of vitamins K and C, folate, and plenty of minerals. Brussels sprouts look like miniature cabbages and have a very similar nutritional content, although they come from a different plant and grow on upright stalks. They have a light, nutty taste when juiced. Cabbage juices taste best when combined with other vegetable juices. Choose firm, tightly packed heads, with no yellowing.

BEST FOR
Antioxidants, for helping to prevent cancer and heart disease.

CALORIES
25/3.5 oz
Brussels sprouts 43/3.5 oz

PREPARATION
Wash the outer leaves and cut into chunks; juice brussels sprouts whole.

Freshly picked cabbage

CARROT

Their fabulous orange color—though purple, yellow, and white varieties are increasingly available—is a clue to the powerful presence of beta-carotene in carrots. A natural antioxidant that helps protect the body from various cancers and can lessen the signs of aging, beta-carotene converts to vitamin A once in the body. We need a regular supply of this vitamin, which is essential for maintaining healthy functioning of the eyes and other parts of the nervous system, as well as keeping the immune system in good working order, and carrots are one of the very best sources. Like many vegetables, carrots are low in calories and full of vitamins and minerals. They make plentiful quantities of sweet, mild-tasting juice that can be drunk on its own or used as a base for mixing with fruits and other vegetables. Look for firm roots that are brightly colored; small roots taste sweeter than older woody ones.

BEST FOR
Beta-carotene, for protection against degenerative disease.

CALORIES
41/3.5 oz

PREPARATION
Cut off any green foliage and scrub the roots; cut into chunks.

CELERY

Celery's crisp, ridged, upright stalks are topped by foliage that looks rather like flat-leaf parsley, though the two plants come from different families. It is a good source of vitamin K, which helps maintain bone density, and the leaves contain vitamin A, for healthy eyes and skin. The antioxidant action of its vitamins is supported by a number of other phytonutrients that have recently been identified and also have an anti-inflammatory role. It contains folate and a good range of minerals in small quantities. Celery has traditionally been eaten as an aid to digestion and is particularly low in calories, making it popular for people on a weight-loss diet. Pregnant women should avoid celery, and it can cause an allergic reaction with anaphylactic shock in some individuals. It has a strong, distinctive taste and is best mixed with other vegetables when juiced. Choose heads with bright, fresh-looking leaves and firm stems.

BEST FOR
Vitamin K, for healthy bones.

CALORIES
16/3.5 oz

PREPARATION
Cut off the bottom end but keep the top foliage, separate the white stalks and wash well.

CUCUMBER

A member of the cucurbit family, which also includes zucchini, melons, and squash, cucumbers have a fairly tough green skin which hides the pale, watery flesh. Given their high moisture content it will be no surprise that cucumbers are very low in calories. The skin is edible and should not be removed when juicing, as it contains most of the cucumber's beneficial nutrients, including beta-carotene, vitamins K and C, and some useful minerals. As well as being a source of antioxidants, cucumber is also thought to have an anti-inflammatory effect, and there is some evidence that its phytonutrients known as lignans may play a part in reducing the risk of cancers of the breast, ovaries, womb, and prostate. Cucumber juice tastes good on its own and is an excellent base for mixing with both fruit and vegetables. Look for vivid color and firm texture when buying. Avoid anything yellowing or flabby.

Fresh cucumber juice

BEST FOR
Potassium, to aid cleansing.

CALORIES
16/3.5 oz

PREPARATION
Wash but don't peel, and cut into chunks.

FENNEL

Topped by a spray of feathery fronds the fennel bulb sits prettily above the ground. It is not a true bulb at all, and its bulbous shape is formed from the swollen bases of its leaf stems. Originally a Mediterranean plant, it smells and tastes of aniseed and is powerfully reminiscent of warm summer evenings in France or Greece. The smell comes from its essential oils, which have some anti-fungal and anti-bacterial effects, so that it is used traditionally as an aid to digestion. It was also one of the herbs in a medicinal mixture that later became the notorious alcoholic drink absinthe. The bulb and its fronds contain useful amounts of antioxidant vitamin C, one of the essential vitamins that keep the body in a good state of repair, as well as some vitamin A and folate, and potassium. The licorice taste can be quite strong and the juice is best mixed with apple or carrot. When buying, choose fresh-looking white bulbs.

BEST FOR
Vitamin C, for healthy blood and bones.

CALORIES
31/3.5 oz

PREPARATION
Remove the tough outer leaves and cut the bulb into chunks.

Fresh fennel juice

KALE

A member of the cabbage family, kale is so nutritious and easy to grow that farmers have traditionally fed it to cattle during the winter. This leafy green vegetable has not had a glamorous past but its reputation has undergone a transformation since it was identified as one of the new superfoods. Packed full of all the healthy nutrients associated with the cabbage family, including beta-carotene, lutein and zeaxanthin, it provides more than the recommended daily intake of vitamins A, C, and K in a single serving and is an important source of calcium and iron. Together, its powerful phytonutrients help prevent cancer and promote healthy eyes, skin, and bones. A winter crop, the leaves should be bought when fresh, crisp, and strongly colored, with no yellowing or wilting. Use without delay, as their nutrient value deteriorates rapidly after harvest. The juice can taste bitter and is best used in small quantities and mixed with other vegetable juices.

Fresh kale juice

BEST FOR
Vitamins A, C, and K for good general health, and calcium for healthy bones.

CALORIES
49/3.5 oz

PREPARATION
Discard any discolored leaves and wash.

LEEK

Although leeks are a member of the onion family, they do not form an obvious bulb but are grown for their thick white stems, which make them look rather like large scallions. Curiously, the seedlings are planted in trenches and covered with soil to prevent the stems turning green. Like onions and garlic, leeks contain a number of significant antioxidants that are known to promote a healthy cardiovascular system, although these tend to be found in smaller quantities in leeks than onions. They are good sources of folate and vitamin A, and contain useful amounts of vitamins K and C, as well as a high level of iron, with other minerals. Like so many vegetables, they are also low in calories. Although leeks taste quite bland when cooked, their juice can be surprisingly strong, and is best added to other juices. When buying, look for firm stems and avoid produce with yellowing tops.

BEST FOR
Antioxidants, for cardiovascular health.

CALORIES
61/3.5 oz

PREPARATION
Remove the stem end and tough outer leaves, wash well to remove grit between the leaf layers and cut into chunks.

LETTUCE

Lettuces come in a bewildering array of shapes and textures, with leaves that may be red or pink rather than the more usual light green, but as a general rule varieties with firmer heads—such as Iceberg—are easier to juice. Lettuce is well known for being low in calories, and frequently forms an important part of a weight-reduction diet, but, like all green leafy vegetables, lettuce is also full of healthy nutrients. It is a great source of beta-carotene and vitamins A and K, with useful amounts of vitamin C and folate. It is also a good source of zeaxanthin, which helps protect the eye, and of iron and manganese. The amount of beta-carotene increases with the amount of color in the lettuce, with red-leaf lettuce like "Lollo Rossa" being the richest source. The leaves can taste bitter when juiced, so you may want to mix them with other fruit and vegetable juices. Avoid buying lettuces with limp or discolored leaves.

BEST FOR
Vitamin A, for healthy eyes.

CALORIES
15/3.5 oz

PREPARATION
Wash and juice whole leaves or cut firmer varieties into chunks.

Mixed lettuce leaves

ONION

This kitchen staple is found in a variety of sizes and colors (usually brown- or red-skinned, but sometimes white) and the underground bulb is made up of modified leaves, rather than being a foodstore for the plant, so it is very low in calories. Beneath the skin the flesh of the bulb is pale-colored. Although it is a useful source of vitamin C, it lacks the healthy complement of other vitamins found in the leafy green vegetables. However, it does contain powerful phytonutrients that more than make up for this. Onions are high in polyphenols and flavonoids, together with other beneficial compounds, which are thought to have a role in protecting the body from cancer, as well as lowering blood sugar levels and helping to reduce the risk of heart disease and stroke. However, you probably need to eat onions on a regular, daily basis in order to receive their full benefit. Choose bulbs that are firm and unbruised.

BEST FOR
Polyphenols, for prevention of cancer and heart disease.

CALORIES
40/3.5 oz

PREPARATION
Remove the papery skin and cut into quarters.

Onions tied together to dry out

PARSLEY

Once upon a time parsley was just a pretty garnish that never got eaten. Times have changed and it has grown up to become an important source of phytonutrients, many of which are particularly helpful to elderly people. With a high content of zeaxanthin for maintaining the aging retina in good health, it is also full of the antioxidant essential vitamins A and C, and particularly rich in vitamin K, which helps keep bones healthy and is thought to limit the damage to the brain caused by Alzheimer's disease. And it has hardly any calories. Flat-leaf parsley has a stronger flavor than the curly-leaf variety, and both types are best drunk in combination with other juices, where they contribute a high dose of nutrients and a lovely shot of color. Look for fresh bunches and avoid any with wilting stems or yellowing leaves. For the ultimate in freshness, try growing your own in a pot by the back door or on a kitchen windowsill.

Parsley growing

BEST FOR
Vitamin K, for healthy bones.

CALORIES
36/3.5 oz

PREPARATION
Wash and juice in handfuls.

Vegetable juice with parsley

PARSNIPS

Parsnips may not have the healthy color of their carrot cousins, but don't let their looks deceive you. Never mind the lack of vitamin A and beta-carotene in these white root vegetables: they have a plentiful supply of other antioxidants which are thought to protect against cancer, particularly of the colon, and are a good source of vitamins C and K, and of folate. They also contain useful amounts of the various minerals that keep the body in good health, such as copper, manganese, and calcium. To retain as many of these vitamins and minerals as possible, leave the skin on the roots but scrub well before juicing to remove any dirt. With a higher sugar content (and calorie count) than carrots, parsnips make a fabulous thick, sweet juice which is best mixed in small quantities with other fruit and vegetable juices. A winter crop, they come into their own when other vegetables are out of season. Look for firm roots that are not too big.

BEST FOR
Antioxidants, for reducing the risk of cancer.

CALORIES
75/3.5 oz

PREPARATION
Scrub the roots and cut into chunks.

PEPPERS

Originating in Central America, where it was discovered by European explorers in the 15th century, the bell pepper has a cheerfully tropical appearance. The gloriously bright colors of ripe bell peppers—red, orange, and yellow—send a clear signal that they are full of beta-carotene. Green peppers are the unripe form, tasting slightly bitter when compared with the brightly colored ripe fruits and containing much lower levels of beneficial nutrients. Beta-carotene has a powerful antioxidant action, giving some protection against cancer, and it converts to vitamin A, which is essential for young-looking skin and healthy eyes. Peppers are also packed with large amounts of antioxidant vitamin C, which boosts the immune system and helps to prevent cancer, as well as lowering the risk of heart disease and strokes. The juice combines well with tomato juice. Buy peppers when they look shiny and unwrinkled, and choose the red, orange, and yellow fruits for higher levels of beta-carotene and vitamin C.

BEST FOR
Vitamin C, for healthy blood and bones.

CALORIES
20/3.5 oz

PREPARATION
Wash and cut open lengthwise, removing the stem, pips, and pith.

Mixed peppers

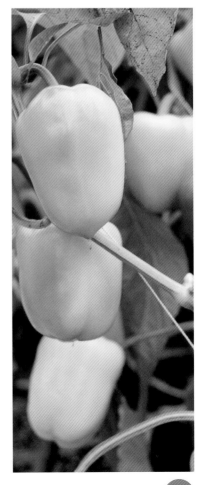

SPINACH

One of the invaluable leafy green vegetables, all of which contain beneficial vitamins and minerals, spinach has endless nutritional virtues, not least that it has very few calories. Its antioxidants beta-carotene and vitamin C help prevent cancer and reduce the risk of heart disease, and plentiful amounts of vitamin A will keep the skin and eyes in good condition. Zeaxanthin is thought to help prevent macular disease in the elderly, and substantial amounts of vitamin K keep bones strong as well as limiting damage to the brain's neurons in people suffering from Alzheimer's disease. Full of iron for healthy red blood cells, spinach is a true superfood with a distinctive peppery taste, and makes a very appealing green juice. A little goes a long way to up the nutrient value of less powerful juices. Choose fresh young leaves where possible, as these have a better flavor, and use them promptly to avoid loss of vitamins.

BEST FOR
Potassium, to regulate the body's water balance.

CALORIES
23/3.5 oz

PREPARATION
Wash leaves and use whole.

Fresh spinach juice

TOMATOES

A distant cousin of the potato and bell pepper, the tomato is now an everyday staple that was originally a native of Central America. Its soft, watery flesh is ideal for juicing, and it is full of highly beneficial nutrients. The brilliant red color indicates the presence of the important antioxidant lycopene (also found in yellow and orange-colored tomatoes), which has an important role to play in reducing the risk of heart disease, and is also thought to help prevent cancers of the prostate, lung, stomach and breast, and protect bones from osteoporosis. The tomato is a rich source of vitamins C, A, and K, all of which are vital for keeping the body functioning well. Inexpensive and abundant, tomatoes make a thick juice with a distinctive taste that mixes well with many fruit and vegetables and is often used as a base. Choose smooth, firm fruits that are a strong, uniform color.

BEST FOR
Lycopene, for healthy bones and muscles.

CALORIES
18/3.5 oz

PREPARATION
Remove the stem and rinse. Cut into halves or quarters to fit into the juicer feed tube.

Fresh tomato juice

71

WATERCRESS

This small-leaved plant is usually grown in beds of running water, and has a strong peppery taste and an abundance of health benefits. Watercress comes from the brassica family, and is a distant relative of the cabbage group. It shares many of the virtues of broccoli and brussels sprouts, being low in calories but rich in antioxidant phytochemicals, vitamins, and minerals. It has been eaten by man for millennia, but has only recently been recognized as one of the superfoods. Its antioxidants, which are believed to have a role in preventing cancer and heart disease, include beta-carotene, lutein and zeaxanthin. It also has good amounts of vitamins K, A, and C, and is a useful source of calcium and iron, for healthy bones and blood. Because it tastes so strong, it is best added to other juices, where it contributes greatly to the flavor and healthiness. Fresh watercress is a deep green color. Avoid leaves that are wilting or yellow.

BEST FOR
Sulphur, to promote healthy skin and hair.

CALORIES
11/3.5 oz

PREPARATION
Remove roots, wash leaves well and use while fresh.

Watercress washed and ready for juicing

WHEATGRASS

This brilliantly colored emerald green juice is certainly a boost to the spirits and its consumption has grown apace in recent years. The nutritional content of wheatgrass is similar to leafy green vegetables, which have an important role in a healthy diet. It contains plenty of vitamin E, and smaller amounts of vitamins A, C, and K, all of which are essential for maintaining the body in good health. It is also a good source of iron. However, anecdotal reports that wheatgrass can reverse cancerous growth and extend life expectancy have not been demonstrated scientifically. Derived from the common wheat plant, wheat seeds can be sown indoors in trays and then harvested when the growth is still green, after as few as ten days, or bought ready-grown. A few individuals may suffer an allergic reaction in the form of facial swelling, throat tightening, or difficulty breathing, soon after drinking wheatgrass juice; these symptoms should be treated as a medical emergency.

BEST FOR
Essential vitamins, for healthy eyes, skin, and bones.

CALORIES
8/1 fl oz juice

PREPARATION
Wash and juice the stalks.

Freshly juiced wheatgrass

KID-FRIENDLY
JUICES

JUICES AND SMOOTHIES AREN'T JUST FOR ADULTS! ALTHOUGH THEY SHOULDN'T BE USED FOR CLEANSING OR DETOXIFYING, OR TO ENCOURAGE WEIGHT LOSS, THEY ARE A GREAT WAY TO INCREASE CONSUMPTION OF FRUITS AND VEGETABLES, AND ENCOURAGE A HEALTHY MINDSET THAT WILL LAST YOUR CHILDREN A LIFETIME.

GETTING YOUR KIDS STARTED ON JUICING

Challenge your children to come up with a wide range of juices by combining different quantities of the following ingredients. Throw in some ginger too!

CARROTS

BERRIES

BEETS

KALE

APPLES

PEACHES

LEMONS

As much as your child may love the fruit juices (and prefer broccoli camouflaged by other ingredients in juice form), resist the temptation to provide too much of the daily nutrition in that fashion. The American Academy of Pediatrics suggests the following guidelines:

No more than half the fruit and vegetable servings for the day should come in juice form.

Juices should never be given to infants under six months old, nor to toddlers who are still drinking from a bottle.

Children 1–4 years old can drink 6 ounces of juice a day; those over the age of 10, up to 12 ounces per day.

All fruits and vegetables should be thoroughly washed before they are juiced.

A selection of berries

ABC VEGGIE DRINK

2 apples
1 beet
2 carrots

Make a game out this recipe by letting your child switch up the order of ingredients to spell different words.

GREEN GREMLIN

2 apples
½ cucumber
½ cup water

Juice apples and cucumber together. Add water to thin the consistency. Settling occurs quickly, so keep a spoon in your cup to stir the drink.

MANGO PEAR

1 mango
1 pear

Peel the mango and cut into pieces before juicing. Juice the mango and the pear. The mango's texture makes this a delicious creamy juice. It has a sweet flavor that kids (and grown-ups) are sure to love. To give it a more tropical flair, stir in or top with shredded coconut.

APPLES, CARROTS & SPINACH

4 apples
2 carrots
1 handful of spinach
½ lemon (optional)

Juice all ingredients; if you are using the press method, blend ingredients in a blender, then send through the press.

ANGEL JUICE

3 apples
½ peeled grapefruit

Core the apple and juice the ingredients together.

CARROT PEAR FENNEL

½ pear
4 carrots
3 fennel stalks
1 celery stalk

Core the pear. Juice the pear, carrots, fennel, and celery.

Fennel

Mango Pear

Angel Juice

Pears

CARROT APPLE GINGER

5 carrots
1 apple
½ inch ginger root

Core the apple and juice the ingredients together.

MANGO PINEAPPLE KALE

1–2 cups loosely packed chopped kale, ribs removed (about 3–4 leaves)
1 mango
1 cup chopped fresh pineapple

Peel and chop the mango before juicing. Juice all the ingredients, beginning with the kale.

GIGGLE JUICE

1 large cucumber
1 thick slice of watermelon

After thoroughly scrubbing all produce, put ingredients through a juicer.

TOMATO CARROT SPINACH APPLE

1 cup spinach
2 carrots
1 tomato
1 apple

Juice all the ingredients, the spinach first because it doesn't yield much juice. This is a great alternative to the commercial bottled and packaged veg-fruit combos and includes a huge serving of spinach!

APPLEDELICIOUS

8 oz apple juice
1 tbsp cucumber juice
1 tbsp pineapple juice.

After thoroughly scrubbing all produce, put ingredients through a juicer.

ORANGE SURPRISE

1 orange
3 carrots
1 apple

After thoroughly scrubbing all produce, put ingredients through a juicer.

GREEN LEMONADE

2 apples
1 lemon
½ head romaine lettuce

After thoroughly scrubbing all produce, put ingredients through a juicer.

MORNING SUN JUICE

2 green apples
4 carrots
1 lemon peeled
1 large handful of spinach

Put all of the ingredients into a blender and blend until smooth.

SHREK OGRE JUICE

2 stalks celery
1 handful kale
3 apples

After thoroughly scrubbing all produce, put ingredients through a juicer.

Carrot Apple Ginger

STRAWBERRY LEMONADE

2½ cups fresh strawberries, rinsed and tops cut off
Juice of 4 lemons
⅓–½ cup sweetener of your choice (depending on how sweet you like it and how sweet your strawberries are)
2 cups cold water
ice

Blend strawberries, lemon juice, and sweetener together in a blender. Pour mixture into a pitcher with 2 cups cold water, and plenty of ice. Stir and let sit for 5–10 minutes. Stir again and serve!

BUNNY JUICE

2 red apples
1 large carrot

After thoroughly scrubbing all produce, put ingredients through a juicer.

X-RAY JUICE

1 orange
3 strawberries
1 lemon
3 carrots
¼ inch ginger root

After thoroughly scrubbing all produce, put ingredients through a juicer.

TIGER JUICE

3 romaine lettuce leaves
2 kale leaves
1 cup spinach
1 handful of baby carrots
1 apple
½ navel orange (or 1 clementine)

Juice greens followed by fruits. Immediately serve in your child's favorite cup and enjoy.

TROPICAL HOP

For a tropical twist, try this delicious juice with hidden veggies!
2 carrots
2 spears of fresh pineapple
dash of lemon juice

After thoroughly scrubbing all produce, put ingredients through a juicer.

GREEN POWER JUICE

1 handful of Swiss chard, kale, spinach, or a combination
1 pear
1 cup strawberries
½ lemon, unpeeled
2 apples

Juice the greens first, followed by the pear, strawberries, lemon, and apple.

Strawberry Lemonade

GREEN GIANT JUICE

2 green apples
2 cucumbers
2 stalks of celery
4–5 kale leaves
1 lemon

After thoroughly scrubbing all produce, put ingredients through a juicer.

GREEN MONSTER JUICE

2 green apples
1 small cucumber
1 handful fresh spinach leaves
¼ inch ginger root
⅛ lemon

After thoroughly scrubbing all produce, put ingredients through a juicer.

WATERMELON LEMONADE

2 pints, seedless watermelon
2 lemons
stevia (to taste)

After thoroughly scrubbing all produce, put ingredients through a juicer.

AUTUMN SUN JUICE

1 apple
1 orange
2 carrots
2 celery stalks
½ lemon

After thoroughly scrubbing all produce, put ingredients through a juicer.

MORNING JUICE

1 pear
1 handful kale
1 apple
2 stalks celery

After thoroughly scrubbing all produce, put ingredients through a juicer.

FRUITY DELIGHT

1 large sweet potato
2 apples
1 large bunch red grapes
1–2 cups of blueberries
3–4 carrots (optional)

After thoroughly scrubbing all produce, put ingredients through a juicer.

Fresh Celery

Watermelon Lemonade

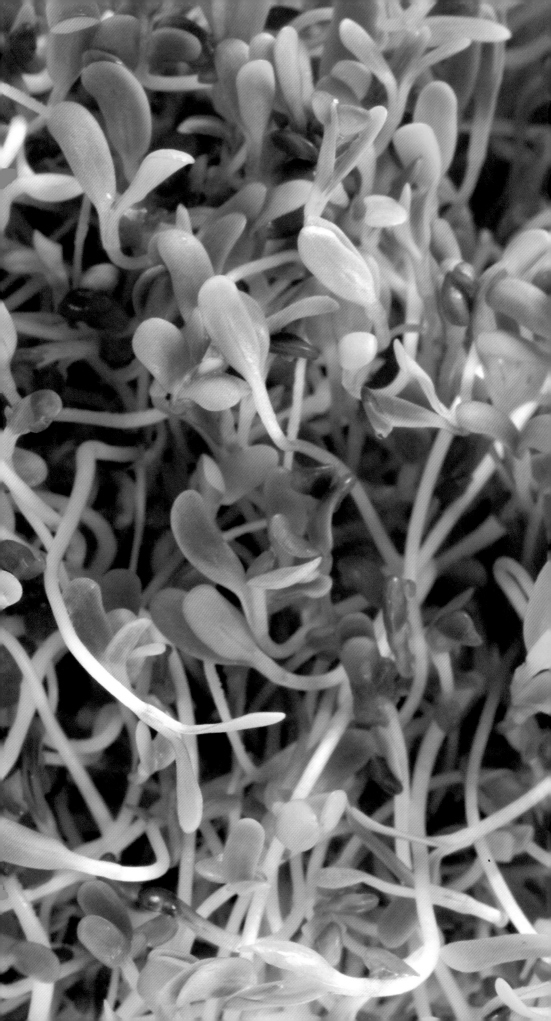

HIGH
ENERGY

FRESH FRUIT AND VEGETABLE JUICES ARE A NATURAL
IN THE ONGOING SEARCH FOR MAXIMUM PHYSICAL
FITNESS, BOTH IN THE GYM AND OUT, AMONG SERIOUS
MARATHONERS AS WELL AS THE WEEKEND ATHLETE.
JUICES HAVE BEEN CREATED TO GIVE THAT MORNING
SURGE BEFORE YOU HEAD FOR THE OFFICE, AND TO BE
USED EITHER BEFORE OR AFTER A WORKOUT.

BLUEBERRY-CABBAGE POWER JUICE

¼ medium red cabbage, sliced

1 large cucumber, peeled and cut into chunks

1 cup fresh blueberries

2 apples

ice cubes (optional)

After thoroughly scrubbing all produce, put ingredients through a juicer.

MORNING RED SUNRISE

1 beet

1 purple carrot

1 cup of strawberries

2 blood oranges

2 celery stalks

Wash all ingredients. Peel the blood oranges and the beet. Chop produce to fit through juicer. Juice all ingredients.

Many versions of this one.
  Substitutions:
Beet: golden beets, carrot: sweet potato

Purple carrot: carrot, sweet potato, golden beets

Strawberries: berries

Blood orange: orange, apple

Celery: cucumber, Celeriac root, lettuce, zucchini, watercress, spinach

SUNBURST JUICE

1 orange

1 red bell pepper

4 carrots

½ lemon

Peel orange and lemon. Wash red pepper. Remove seeds and stem. Wash carrots. Juice all ingredients. Pour over ice.

GET UP & GO

4 small carrots

1 cucumber

1 apple

1 beet, thinly peeled

½-inch piece fresh ginger

After washing all produce, put ingredients through a juicer.

GO GREEN

6–8 leaves kale

3 small apples

1 cucumber, peeled

2–3 stalks celery

½ lemon (no peel)

2 inches fresh ginger

1 cup water

After thoroughly scrubbing all produce, put ingredients through a juicer.

ROADRUNNER

1 cup alfalfa sprouts

1 whole red cabbage

1 large cucumber

10–12 grapes

After thoroughly washing all produce, put ingredients through a juicer.

Morning Red Sunrise

VIBRANT GINGER TONIC

2 lemons, peeled
2-inch chunk ginger, peeled
4 large stalks of celery (stems and leaves)
pinch of pink sea salt
Sweet ingredient: 1 small green apple or 2 tsp agave/maple syrup
dash of cayenne (optional)

Juice the lemon and ginger separately. Place juice aside. Juice the celery or celery/apple blend. Pour 1-2 parts ginger/lemon blend in each glass. Then add 5 parts green juice. Customize the ratio however you'd like, though. Swirl in some maple/agave syrup for sweetness if you did not include an apple in your juice.

Add a dash of optional cayenne on top.

MORNING BOOST JUICE

1 small-medium pink grapefruit, peeled
1 apple
3 carrots
1 tsp fresh ginger, peeled
½ lemon, peeled

After thoroughly scrubbing all produce, put ingredients through a juicer.

CARROTS, CUCUMBERS, APPLE, BEET & GINGER

1 cucumber, peeled
3 carrots, scrubbed well, tops removed, ends trimmed
1 beet, scrubbed well, with stem and 1 or 2 leaves
2 stalks celery
1 handful parsley
1- or 2-inch chunk ginger root scrubbed, or peeled if old
½ lemon, peeled

After washing all produce, put ingredients through a juicer.

Fresh broccoli and carrots

TEN MINUTE SUNRISE

2 grapefruits (peeled)
1 red bell pepper
2 pears
5 carrots

After washing all produce, put ingredients through a juicer.

GREEN MAGI

2 celery stalks
2 cucumbers
4 kale leaves

After thoroughly scrubbing all produce, put ingredients through a juicer.

THE MORNING DRIVE

1 stalk broccoli
5 carrots

After thoroughly scrubbing all produce, put ingredients through a juicer.

The Morning Drive

HIGH ENERGY JUICE

6 carrots
4 celery stalks
½ bunch cilantro
2 tomatoes
1 lemon

After thoroughly scrubbing all produce, put ingredients through a juicer.

KALE ENERGY BOOSTER

1 cup kale
1 cucumber
1 apple
½ bunch of parsley
3 carrots

After thoroughly scrubbing all produce, put ingredients through a juicer.

THE FAB FIVE

2 celery stalks, leaves included

1 carrot, green top removed

1 leaf green cabbage

1 leaf chard (Swiss, rainbow, green, or red)

4 leaves kale

3 stems parsley

½ cucumber, peeled

½ lemon

½ apple

After washing all produce, put ingredients through a juicer.

COCONUT SPLASH

½ cantaloupe, peeled
8 oz coconut water

After thoroughly scrubbing all produce, put ingredients through a juicer.

BAZINGO

1 lemon
2 bunches parsley
2 apples
4-inch piece of ginger
4 carrots

After washing all produce, put ingredients through a juicer.

Bazingo

Coconut Splash

SUNSET BLEND

1 large sweet potato
2 small carrots
1 red bell pepper
2 large red beets
2 apples

After washing all produce, put ingredients through a juicer.

RAINBOW JUICE

5 celery stalks
½ medium cucumber
2 carrots
1 medium tomato
½ medium orange
½ medium peach

After thoroughly scrubbing all produce, put ingredients through a juicer.

NIGHTTIME ENERGY DRINK

5 carrots
2 celery stalks
1 cup parsley

After thoroughly scrubbing all produce, put ingredients through a juicer.

Sunset Blend

Carrots and sweet potatoes

Nighttime Energy Drink

NATURAL ENERGY

1½ cups coconut water
2 cups spinach
1 cup kale
2 celery stalks
1 banana
1–2 tbsp cinnamon

After thoroughly scrubbing all produce, blend all ingredients until smooth in a blender.

BATTERY BOOSTER

4 carrots
1 clove garlic
1 tsp ginseng powder

After scrubbing the carrots, juice first the carrots and then the garlic; add the ginseng powder to the fresh carrot and garlic juice.

JUICY PRE-WORKOUT

3 apples
3–4 leaves kale
a bunch of romaine lettuce
a bunch of cilantro
¼ lemon
a few leaves of mint
1 inch ginger (optional)

After thoroughly scrubbing all produce, put ingredients through a juicer.

GOLDEN SPICY BEET JUICE

1 large or 2 small golden beets
3 small carrots
1 pear
1 large orange, peeled
½ inch ginger, peeled
garnish: 3 dashes of cayenne, slice of raw beet (optional)

After thoroughly scrubbing all produce, put ingredients through a juicer.

Fresh Kale

Juicy Pre-workout

TURNIPS AND FENNEL

½ turnip
3 carrots
1 apple
¼ fennel bulb

After thoroughly scrubbing all produce, put ingredients through a juicer.

POWER POST-WORKOUT JUICE

½ head of romaine lettuce
4 leaves kale
4 carrots
½ bunch carrot tops
2 small apples
1 lime

After thoroughly scrubbing all produce, put ingredients through a juicer.

JUICY POST-WORKOUT

2 green apples
1 celery stalk
1 small cucumber
2 tomatoes
1 orange

After thoroughly scrubbing all produce, put ingredients through a juicer.

LEMONS, PEARS, CELERY & CUCUMBER

1 pear
2 celery stalks
1 cup water
juice of ½ lemon
1 cucumber
¼ tsp salt
¼ tsp pepper

After washing all produce, put ingredients through a juicer.

PARSLEY POWER

1 large bunch of parsley
2 carrots
1 apple
1 celery stalk

After thoroughly scrubbing all produce, put ingredients through a juicer.

Lemons, Pears, Celery & Cucumber

Parsley Power

CLEANSING
JUICES

CLEANSING ROUTINES COMBINE CERTAIN JUICES
FOR DIFFERENT SYSTEMS IN THE BODY WITH DIET
REGIMENS OVER A SPECIFIED LENGTH OF TIME. SOME
TARGET INDIVIDUAL SYSTEMS IN THE BODY, WHETHER
DIGESTIVE OR HEPATIC, WHILE OTHERS—THE MASTER
CLEANSERS AT THE BEGINNING OF THIS CHAPTER—
WAGE AN ATTACK ON ALL FRONTS. MANY PROVIDE
THE FIRST STEP FOR SUCCESSFUL WEIGHT LOSS BY
CLEANSING YOUR BODY BEFORE YOU EMBARK ON A
NEW LIFE OF HEALTHIER FOODS.

CLEANSERS

Think of cleansers as an invigorating way of doing a spring cleaning of your body—not unlike that much-needed spring cleaning of your home, armed with vacuum, dust cloths, and trash bags! Spring-cleaning your home may be a matter of choice. Spring-cleaning and detoxifying your body is not.

Over time and as the result of many bad habits, your system gets clogged, affecting the many processes that clean your body. Your kidneys become less efficient in purifying the blood. The ability of the liver—the metabolism powerhouse that processes, stores, or manufactures most of the chemicals passing through your body—to detoxify your system and produce bile to break up fats, is reduced. The digestive tract, from mouth to colon, digests food and moves the unused wastes out of the body—but the highly processed foods so common in our diet today can take days to digest. And the wastes that build up in the colon need to be flushed out. A malfunctioning system reveals itself in the health and vitality of our skin, hair, and breath.

Fresh beet

Pineapple and coconut juice

CLEANSERS

Certain cleansing routines involve consumption of only a single juice over a week or more and no solid food, and are known as juice fasts; these may work for people who want to clear their system and start losing weight quickly. Other fasting regimens use a variety of juices that target different systems over a shorter period of time, and these juices can either be part of a juice fast or used with other foods or juices in a juice-heavy diet. You should always discuss a juice fast with your doctor because the imbalance caused by omitting some food groups and concentrating on others may exacerbate certain medical conditions.

Detoxifying regimens need not be onerous: your favorite juices can serve as powerful cleansers. Fresh fruit and vegetables supply everything needed to detoxify, and can be mixed in various combinations. See the following pages for suggestions on jump-starting your healthy, reinvigorated life in a new body!

Apple and mint

Cucumber, lemon, and ginger juice

A 5-DAY ALKALINE INCORPORATES A WIDE VARIETY OF JUICES, OF WHICH THE FOLLOWING RECIPES ARE JUST A SMALL SAMPLE:

CUCUMBER FENNEL

1 cucumber
a piece of fennel
1 lemon, peeled
1 stalk celery

After thoroughly scrubbing all produce, put ingredients through a juicer.

DRINK YOUR VEGGIES

2 pears
1 inch ginger
4 medium carrots
3 celery stalks
1 baby beet
½ cup parsley (stems and leaves)
2 tsp fresh lemon juice

After thoroughly scrubbing all produce, put ingredients through a juicer.

SUPER-GREEN CLEANSER

8 kale leaves
2 large handfuls of parsley
1 large cucumber
3 celery stalks (plus leaves)
1 zucchini
½ lime

Wash all vegetables. Peel lime for a less bitter flavor. Add produce through your juicer and enjoy.

GREEN CLEAN

1 cucumber
2 apples
1 bunch kale
a few large handfuls of spinach
1 lemon, peeled

After thoroughly scrubbing all produce, put ingredients through a juicer.

GREEN ALFALFA

2 big handfuls of spinach
3 stalks celery
1 little gem lettuce
1 small green pepper
½ cucumber
a handful of alfalfa sprouts

After thoroughly scrubbing all produce, put ingredients through a juicer.

HEARTBEET

1 beet
3 small apples
1 pear
½ inch ginger
juice of ½ lemon

After thoroughly scrubbing all produce, put ingredients through a juicer.

Heartbeet

LIMONADE DIET

2 tbsp fresh-squeezed lime juice

2 tbsp grade-B organic maple syrup

a pinch of cayenne pepper

10 oz filtered water

Mix the ingredients in a large glass. Drink six or more servings a day, a saltwater flush of 2 tsp salt in a quart of water in the morning, and an herbal laxative tea at night for ten days. This lemonade fast was created by Stanley Burroughs over 50 years ago.

SCARLET RHAPSODY

1 green apple

½ large cucumber

½ medium beet

½ inch ginger (optional)

Process all ingredients through a juicer. If you are using it as part of a juice fast, strain it and dilute with an equal quantity of filtered water. If not fasting, you can consume it unstrained.

IN THREES

3 cucumbers

3 cups spinach

3 cups parsley

3 celery stalks

1 lemon

After thoroughly washing all produce, put ingredients through a juicer.

BROCCOLI, CARROT & PARSLEY

2 handfuls of broccoli

1 handful of parsley

3 carrots

2 apples

a little bit of flaxseed oil

After thoroughly scrubbing all produce, put ingredients through a juicer.

RED DAWN CLEANSER

1 apple

3 leaves kale

1 beet

a large bunch of red grapes

¼ red cabbage

½ inch giner

After thoroughly washing all produce, put ingredients through a juicer.

APPLE CLEANSE

This is one of the very few cleansing routines that is not juice based. However, because it operates on the same principles, it has been included here.

Eat as many apples as you want—any time you're hungry instead of snacks or regular meals—and drink only lukewarm water all day. This cleanse is done for just three days at a time.

Scarlet Rhapsody

BERRY CLEANSER

2 large apples
½ lime
4 cups strawberries

After thoroughly scrubbing all produce, put ingredients through a juicer.

CARROT, APPLE, LEMON

3 medium carrots
2 apples
½ lemon

After thoroughly scrubbing all produce, put ingredients through a juicer.

CELERY PARSLEY DETOX

1 medium apple
½ beet
3 medium carrots
2 stalks celery
1 handful of parsley

After thoroughly scrubbing all produce, put ingredients through a juicer.

Carrot, Apple, Lemon

Berry Cleanser

APPLE JUICE SPRING CLEAN

One of the simplest colon cleansers doesn't necessitate a juicer at all. Start the day with a large glass of unfiltered prune juice. Follow this with a large glass of water at room temperature. Then alternate between apple juice and water every half hour throughout the day.

FRESH NINE CLEANSING JUICE

3 beets
4 carrots
3 celery stalks
3 cucumbers
3 lemons, peeled
3 handfuls of lettuce
3 handfuls of parsley
3 handfuls of kale
2 inch ginger

Wash all ingredients carefully and juice together. This recipe should produce enough juice to drink one 8-ounce glass every hour, for eight hours. Add extra cucumber if required.

COLON CLEANSER

3 handfuls of spinach
4 green apples
2 handfuls of parsley (optional)

Juice together apples and spinach and, if desired, parsley.
   Drink one cup every four hours, unstrained for maximum benefit.

Freshly sliced ginger

Fresh Nine Cleansing Juice

TWISTY FRUIT PUNCH

3 medium apples
4 kiwis
¼ lemon, with rind
¼ lime, with rind
2 oranges, peeled
1 pineapple, peeled and cored

Process all ingredients in a juicer, shake or stir, and serve.

VEGETABLE DETOX JUICE

4 carrots
4 kale leaves
3 celery stalks
2 beets
1 turnip
½ bunch of spinach
½ cabbage
½ bunch of parsley
½ onion
2 garlic cloves
$\frac{1}{10}$ tsp cayenne powder

Mix all ingredients with water and puree in a blender.

THE BELLY CLEANSER

5 carrots
2 apples
12 spinach leaves

After thoroughly scrubbing all produce, put ingredients through a juicer.

DETOX

2 tbsp peeled and chopped fresh ginger

1 medium beet, scrubbed and coarsely chopped

4 medium carrots, scrubbed and sliced

1 medium apple, cored and cubed (3 inches dia.)

1 cup water

In a blender, combine ginger, beet, carrots, apple, and water; blend, scraping down sides occasionally, until smooth. Strain juice and, if desired, thin with additional water.

Freshly sliced kiwifruit

The Belly Cleanser

APPLE, BEET & CARROT

1 beet, rinsed, lightly peeled, and quartered

1 apple, lighted peeled, cored and quartered

1 inch ginger, peeled

4 carrots, rinsed and peeled

unfiltered apple juice (optional)

Place all ingredients in a blender and blend until smooth, adding a splash of apple juice if needed

Then, place a fine mesh strainer over a large bowl and pour the juice over. Use a rubber spatula to press the pulp down and squeeze all of the juice out. Let stand for 5 minutes so you get most of the juice.

Discard pulp and pour your juice into a serving glass. Drink immediately or chill for a bit. Will keep in the refrigerator for a day or so, but will taste best when fresh.

LIVER CLEANSER

1 large apple

1 beet

4 carrots

1 celery stalk

½ inch ginger

After thoroughly scrubbing all produce, put ingredients through a juicer.

THE SUPER SALAD

1 cucumber

1 lemon

1 medium green onion/ scallion

1 handful of parsley

½ medium sweet red pepper

3 small tomatoes

After thoroughly scrubbing all produce, put ingredients through a juicer.

Strawberries

HIPSTER BEET

2 whole beets, small

2 cups strawberries

1 cup cherries

1 cup cranberries

After thoroughly scrubbing all produce, put ingredients through a juicer.

PIZZA PARTY

½ head medium cauliflower

1 small cucumber

2 cups cherry tomatoes

dash of dried basil

After thoroughly washing all produce, put ingredients through a juicer.

CELERY COOLER

2 large celery stalks

1 handful of cilantro

1 small cucumber

1 medium tomato

Juice tomato, celery, cucumber, and cilantro in that order.

Hipster Beet

SPICY RED TANG

1 beet
3 large carrots
2 large stalks celery
1 inch ginger, peeled
½ lime
1 jalapeño pepper
2 cups spinach

After thoroughly washing all produce, put ingredients through a juicer.

TO THE BEET OF YOUR HEART

1 beet
2 leaves red cabbage
4 small carrots
½ lemon
1 orange
¼ pineapple
2 handfuls of spinach

After thoroughly washing all produce, put ingredients through a juicer.

JUST BEET IT

2 medium apples
1 beet
6 small carrots
3 large stalks celery
1 small cucumber
½ inch ginger

After thoroughly scrubbing all produce, put ingredients through a juicer.

Ingredients for Just Beet It

Just Beet It

SUMMER MELON

1 medium tomato

1 large wedge of watermelon (approx ⅛ of melon)

After thoroughly scrubbing all produce, put ingredients through a juicer.

PINEBERRY CLEANSER

½ large pineapple, peeled, cored, and cut into cubes

2 cups strawberries

1 pear

25 mint leaves

After thoroughly scrubbing all produce, put ingredients through a juicer.

SPRING CLEAN

½ lemon

3 tomatoes

1 large wedge of watermelon (approx ⅛ of melon)

1 handful of parsley

After thoroughly scrubbing all produce, put ingredients through a juicer.

YOSEMITE FALLS CLEANSER

1 wedge watermelon

½ pound red grapes

After thoroughly scrubbing all produce, put ingredients through a juicer.

Summer Melon

Pineberry Cleanser

LUNG POWER CLEANSING JUICE

Head of celery
2–4 Fuji apples
1 lemon
½ inch ginger
1 bunch of wild watercress

After thoroughly scrubbing all produce, put ingredients through a juicer.

SUMMER COOLER

2 medium apples
5 Swiss chard leaves
6 celery stalks
1 bunch parsley
1 lemon, peeled
½ inch ginger
1 inch turmeric
watermelon rind (at least 2 rinds)

After thoroughly scrubbing all produce, put ingredients through a juicer.

RADIANT RADISH CLEANSER

1 large radish
2 apples
1 pear
½ jicama
1 lime, peeled
1 handful of cilantro
pinch of sea salt, optional

After thoroughly scrubbing all produce, put ingredients through a juicer.

Fresh lime and cilantro

Lung Power Cleansing Juice

CUCUMBER, CELERY, MINT, APPLE & PINEAPPLE

1 cucumber
2 celery stalks
2 green apples
2 pineapple slices
1 cup mint leaves

After thoroughly scrubbing all produce, put ingredients through a juicer.

PERFECT SKIN JUICE

½ bunch spinach
½ bunch celery
½ large cucumber
1 head romaine lettuce
⅓ bunch fresh parsley
pinch of Himalayan salt

After thoroughly scrubbing all produce, put ingredients through a juicer.

RED PEPPER SKIN CLEANSER

2 red peppers
2 carrots
1 apple
1 broccoli spear

After thoroughly scrubbing all produce, put ingredients through a juicer.

Red Pepper Skin Cleanser

Cucumber, Celery, Mint, Apple & Pineapple

JUICE
REMEDIES

NOT ONLY ARE JUICES USED AS CLEANSERS TO
PURGE AND PURIFY THE SYSTEM, OR AS HEALTHFUL
ALTERNATIVES TO A JUNK-LADEN DIET, THEY
ALSO PROVIDE COMMON SENSE HEALTH BENEFITS
AND RELIEF FROM THE SYMPTOMS OF COMMON
AILMENTS THROUGH THEIR ACTIVE INGREDIENTS—
FROM CARROTS, BEETS, AND PARSLEY, TO APPLES
AND CITRUS FRUITS. WHETHER YOUR PROBLEM IS
ALLERGIES OR ARTHRITIS, INSOMNIA OR MIGRAINES,
CONSIDER THESE RECIPES FOR A DELICIOUS AND
HEALTHFUL SOLUTION.

REMEDIES

The curative powers of a wide range of vegetable and fruit products have been recognized for centuries, from the use of pomegranate juice in Ancient Greece as an aphrodisiac, to the combination of pomegranates and figs as an elixir to promote physical strength and prowess, recorded in the Dead Sea Scrolls. Spaniards planted the first Florida orange trees in the 1500s, but it wasn't until the early 20th century that pasteurization coupled with the transcontinental railroad provided orange juice across the country as a popular breakfast beverage.

Juicing as a nutritional and alternative treatment took off after home juicers were invented in the 1950s, making it possible to create juice combinations with a wide range of healthful effects in your own kitchen so that you could consume the juice as soon as you made it. In more recent years, a wide range of juice bars will create anything on request, and even the corner café has a juicer and can offer a fresh carrot juice. In addition, there are many commercially prepared juices on the market, so even if you don't have your own kitchen equipment, you can obtain one of the commercially prepared juices to help ease your symptoms.

Fresh figs

Freshly squeezed orange juice

REMEDIES

If you are under medical supervision for an existing condition, juices should be used only as complementary therapies to your regular treatment until you have established whether they work for you. And you should never attempt to replace medical treatment with juicing until you have discussed it with your physician. Certain ingredients—for example, grapefruit juice—have a well-established capacity for interfering with the metabolism of prescribed treatments, bringing them to a toxic level. Fruit juices, higher in natural sugar than whole fruits and without the fiber, can cause a spike in blood sugar level, so vegetable juices can be safer for people with diabetes.

Other ingredients are natural panaceas for a host of different symptoms and conditions, and the Nutrition Benefits section (p.24–73) details some of the many different benefits of each ingredient. For example, it has been found that daily consumption of apples and apple juice protects against asthma and increases bone density, while lemon juice helps control high blood pressure and respiratory disorders. Explore the following pages to find juices that will stop a migraine in its tracks, or will help relieve acid reflux.

Lemon juice with sliced lemons

Freshly squeezed apple juice

PARSLEY LEMONADE

2 cups flat-leaf parsley
1 small cucumber
2 lemons, peeled
1 green apple
1 inch ginger (optional)
1 tsp honey

After thoroughly washing all produce, put ingredients through a juicer.

MINUS-SINUS RELIEVER

1 large orange, peeled
½ lemon, de-seeded and peeled
1 apple
1 inch ginger, peeled
cayenne spice

After thoroughly scrubbing all produce, put ingredients through a juicer.

GINGER SHOOTER

1 large pear
1 inch ginger, peeled
1 tangerine
1 tbsp fresh squeezed lemon juice

After thoroughly scrubbing all produce, put ingredients through a juicer.

DANDELION LEAF RELIEF

2 cups fresh dandelion greens or 6 leaves (not the flowers)
5 celery stalks
1 cup spinach
2 cucumbers
2 apples
1 lime or lemon
½ inch ginger (optional)

After thoroughly scrubbing all produce, put ingredients through a juicer.

VITA-JUICE

3 large red beets
4 small carrots
2 celery stalks
4 plum tomatoes
4 cups parsley, roughly chopped
1 jalapeño, ribs and seeds removed
8 red radishes

After thoroughly washing all produce, put ingredients through a juicer.

JAPPLE GINGER JUICE

5 jazz apples
½-1 lemon, peeled
1 inch ginger, peeled
dash of cayenne (optional)

After thoroughly scrubbing all produce, put ingredients through a juicer.

Vita-juice

BEET IT
1 beet
1 clove of garlic
2 apples

After thoroughly scrubbing all produce, put ingredients through a juicer.

MOHEETO
2 limes
1 inch ginger
4 mint leaves

After thoroughly washing all produce, put ingredients through a juicer.
   Sip this mixture with some water for the soothing and heating properties of ginger and cleansing benefits of limes.

HART-2-BEET
1 beet
2 apples
1 pear
1 inch ginger
½ lemon

After thoroughly scrubbing all produce, put ingredients through a juicer.

RED DEVIL
2 small beets
2-inch piece of ginger
3 cucumbers
½ lemon

After thoroughly scrubbing all produce, put ingredients through a juicer.

THE ORANGE GENIE
3 small apples
12 small carrots
1 large orange

After thoroughly scrubbing all produce, put ingredients through a juicer.

Mint leaves

Moheeto

BLUEBERRY BREEZE

3 leaves basil (fresh)
1½ cups blueberries
2 pinches cayenne
pepper (spice)
½ lime
5 cups diced
watermelon

After thoroughly scrubbing
all produce, put ingredients
through a juicer.

MELON TEA

1 large wedge
watermelon
½ cup green tea, chilled
½ lemon

After thoroughly scrubbing
all produce, put ingredients
through a juicer.

HANG ON

1 beet
3 large celery stalks
3 cups spinach
1 tsp Spirulina (dried)

After washing all produce, put
ingredients through a juicer.

JAZZY GINGER ZINGER

2 green apples
3 small carrots
½ inch ginger
½ lemon (with rind)

After washing all produce, put
ingredients through a juicer.

Jazzy Ginger Zinger

Blueberry Breeze

MINTY BERRY

2 cups blueberries
2 kiwis, peeled
20 strawberries
2 cups mint leaves

After thoroughly washing
all produce, put ingredients
through a juicer.

SUPER BLOOD-BOOST

1 bunch spinach
1 bunch organic parsley
handful of Swiss chard
½ lemon, peeled and
seeded (or to taste)

After thoroughly scrubbing
all produce, put ingredients
through a juicer.

THE IRON LADY

1 bunch spinach
1 bunch parsley
handful of Swiss chard
1 apple, cored
½ inch ginger

After thoroughly scrubbing
all produce, put ingredients
through a juicer.

Super Blood-boost

Minty Berry

GOLDFINGER

1 golden beet
1 pear
3 large carrots
4 large celery stalks
1 small cucumber
½ inch ginger

After thoroughly scrubbing all produce, put ingredients through a juicer.

BREAST CANCER ELIXIR

½ lemon
1 large whole tomato
1 large wedge of watermelon (approx ⅛ of melon)

After thoroughly scrubbing all produce, put ingredients through a juicer.

GOOD & GREEN

2 large Green apples
8 large stalks celery
1 lemon with peel)
1 small tangerine, peeled

After thoroughly scrubbing all produce, put ingredients through a juicer.

DRAGON FIRE

4 leaves red cabbage
½ lemon with rind
3 small pears

After thoroughly scrubbing all produce, put ingredients through a juicer.

TANGO IN THE TROPICS

2 peaches, pits removed
2 pears
½ pineapple

After thoroughly scrubbing all produce, put ingredients through a juicer.

STRAWBERRY, PINEAPPLE, MINT

1 pear
15 leaves peppermint
½ pineapple
15 strawberries

After thoroughly scrubbing all produce, put ingredients through a juicer.

Strawberry, Pineapple, Mint

SOUR CHERRY-POMEGRANATE JUICE

2 cups sour cherries

1 pomegranate, skin removed

1 apple, core removed

After thoroughly scrubbing all produce, put ingredients through a juicer.

ASPARAGUS SOOTHER

2 small apples

4 medium asparagus spears

1 stalk broccoli

4 carrots

3 celery stalks

1 tbsp olive oil (extra virgin)

1 handful of parsley

After thoroughly scrubbing all produce, put ingredients through a juicer.

APPLE GINGER JUICE

3 curly kale leaves with stems, coarsely chopped

4 sprigs flat-leaf parsley

2 green apples, cored, and coarsely chopped

1 inch ginger, coarsely chopped

1 teaspoon fresh lemon juice, plus more to taste

½ tsp honey

Pass the kale, parsley, apples, and ginger through a juicer, discarding the solids. Mix in the lemon juice and honey, adjusting with more juice and honey to taste. Serve immediately.

CARROT, GINGER, APPLE

¼ inch fresh ginger

4 carrots, greens removed

2 apples, seeds removed

After thoroughly scrubbing all produce, put ingredients through a juicer.

BROCCOLI CARROT

½ cup fresh broccoli, cut in pieces

3 medium carrots, roots only

1 apple, core removed

½ lemon, peeled

After washing all produce, put ingredients through a juicer.

Pomegranates on wooden table

Sour Cherry-Pomegranate Juice

PEACH & PLUM

4 plums
3 peaches
2 apricots

Remove pits and juice. Softer, ripe plums, peaches, and apricots produce more of a puree than juice.

CARROT CLEANSER

1 medium apple
4 medium carrots
2 celery stalks
1 small cucumber
½ inch ginger

After thoroughly scrubbing all produce, put ingredients through a juicer.

THE LEMON MOVER

2 apples
8 medium carrots
1 inch ginger
1 lemon

After thoroughly scrubbing all produce, put ingredients through a juicer.

FRUIT PUNCH

4 apples
4 kiwis
½ lime
2 oranges, peeled
1 pineapple

After thoroughly scrubbing all produce, put ingredients through a juicer.

SWEET SOOTHER

2 apples
2 beets
2 carrots
1 red pepper
1 sweet potato
1 small celery stalk
½ cucumber
½ inch ginger

After washing all produce, put ingredients through a juicer.

Freshly picked celery

Sweet Soother

CARROTS & CELERY

4 stalks of celery
2 large carrots
1 large apple

After thoroughly scrubbing all produce, put ingredients through a juicer.

SPINACH CARROT JUICE

1½ cup filtered water or coconut water
½ cup pineapple
1 cup spinach
4 carrots
1 cup ice

Place all ingredients into the blender in the order listed, secure lid, and blend until smooth.

CARROT, BEET & GINGER JUICE

1 large or 2 medium beets, cut into wedges
½ lemon, zest and pith removed
2 large carrots
1 large apple, cut into wedges
1 inch ginger

After thoroughly scrubbing all produce, put ingredients through a juicer.

CARROT, CRANBERRY & BLUEBERRY JUICE

2 carrots
1 cup cranberries
1 cup blueberries

After washing all produce, put ingredients through a juicer.

Coconut water

Spinach Carrot Juice

Carrot, Beet & Ginger Juice

GUT EASE

2 pears
2 carrots
½ pineapple
½ inch ginger

After thoroughly scrubbing all produce, put ingredients through a juicer.

WHEATGRASS AND GINGER JUICE

1 bunch of wheatgrass (about a handful)
1 lemon
4 apples
2 carrots
2-inch piece of ginger

After thoroughly scrubbing all produce, put ingredients through a juicer.

THE GREEN DOCTOR

2 cups spinach
¼ cucumber
¼ head of celery
1 bunch of parsley
1 bunch of mint
4 carrots
2 apples
¼ orange
¼ lime
¼ lemon
¼ pineapple

After thoroughly scrubbing all produce, put ingredients through a juicer.

Gut Ease

The Green Doctor

GREEN EXTINGUISHER

2 green apples
1 lemon, peeled
½ inch ginger
1½ large English cucumbers
2–3 broccoli stems
handful of leftover kale stems

After thoroughly scrubbing all produce, put ingredients through a juicer.

BLUEBERRY & APPLE

2 cups of blueberries
1 apple

After thoroughly scrubbing all produce, put ingredients through a juicer.

TROPICAL DELIGHT

1 papaya
1 guava
2 mangos

After thoroughly scrubbing all produce, put ingredients through a juicer.

Sliced cucumber

ALKALINE FIREFIGHTER

½ cucumber
1 cup of spinach
1 cup of kale
1 cup of parsley
½ apple

After thoroughly scrubbing all produce, put ingredients through a juicer.

MAGIC ALKALINE GREENS

1 cup of broccoli heads
2 stalks of celery (including leaves)
4 large carrots
1-inch slice of fresh ginger (optional)

After thoroughly scrubbing all produce, put ingredients through a juicer.

ALKALINE PARADISE

1 cup of spinach
½ cucumber
2 celery stalks (including leaves)
4 carrots
½ apple

After thoroughly scrubbing all produce, put ingredients through a juicer.

Alkaline Paradise

GINGER NINJA

3 green apples
2 celery sticks
1 large cucumber or 2 smaller cucumbers
1 lime
2-inch piece of ginger

After thoroughly scrubbing all produce, put ingredients through a juicer.

Substitutions:
Green apple: other varieties of apple, pear
Celery: zucchini, lettuce, fennel
Cucumber: celery, zucchini, lettuce
Lime: grapefruit, lemon
Ginger: mint

SPICY BEET JUICE

½–1 small beet
1 small carrot
¼ yellow bell pepper
2 lemon wedges, with rind
2 large romaine lettuce leaves
Jalapeño pepper and cilantro according to taste

After thoroughly scrubbing all produce, put ingredients through a juicer.

BETTER DIGESTION

1 cucumber
½ lemon
1 spring onion
1 handful parsley
1 small red pepper
3 small whole tomatoes

After thoroughly scrubbing all produce, put ingredients through a juicer.

DIGESTION AID

1 cucumber
1 medium fennel bulb
1 handful fresh mint leaves
1 inch ginger
2 celery stalks
1 apple (optional)

After thoroughly scrubbing all produce, put ingredients through a juicer.

Ginger Ninja

Better Digestion

GREEK GODDESS JUICE

1 pear
2 celery stalks
3 kale leaves
½ avocado
1½ green apples
1½ cup water
juice of 1 lime
1 cucumber, peeled and deseeded
¼ tsp salt
¼ tsp pepper
⅛ tsp chat masala/ cumin powder

After thoroughly scrubbing all produce, put ingredients through a juicer.

PINEBERRY SURPRISE

½ pineapple
1 handful cranberries
1 handful strawberries
8 tbsp pineapple juice

After thoroughly scrubbing all produce, put ingredients through a juicer.

GREEN GRAPEFRUIT

4 large kale leaves
2 handfuls spinach
2 sticks celery
1 grapefruit, peeled

After thoroughly scrubbing all produce, put ingredients through a juicer.

CARROT DIGESTIF

5 carrots
½ pineapple
2 large white cabbage leaves

After thoroughly scrubbing all produce, put ingredients through a juicer.

SUPERB DEFENDER

5 large kale leaves
4 carrots
1 orange

After thoroughly scrubbing all produce, put ingredients through a juicer.

Pears

Pineberry Surprise

GREEN BEANS & BRUSSELS SPROUTS

1 cup string beans
6 brussels sprouts
1 lemon, peeled

After thoroughly scrubbing all produce, put ingredients through a juicer.

SPINACH & CELERY JUICE

3 green apples
2 stalks celery
large bunch of baby spinach.

After scrubbing clean all produce, juice some of the spinach first. Then, alternate among celery, apples and spinach, to help flush spinach out of the juicer. Makes two glasses, one to enjoy now and one for later.

FRENCH GREEN BEANS & BRUSSELS SPROUTS

1 cup French green beans
8 brussels sprouts
1 lemon, peeled

After thoroughly scrubbing all produce, put ingredients through a juicer.

GREEN CARROT JUICE

6 spinach leaves
1 handful parsley
2 stalks celery
5 carrots

Thoroughly scrub all produce and peel the carrots. Juice all ingredients together.

SPEARED APPLE JUICE

2 green apples
6 asparagus spears

Wash produce thoroughly, then juice apples and asparagus spears together.

WATERCRESS, TOMATOES & PARSLEY JUICE

3 stalks celery
3 tomatoes
1 small bunch fresh parsley
1 handful of watercress
½ lemon

Thoroughly clean all produce, then juice them together.

Asparagus spears

Green Beans & Brussel Sprouts

BROCCOLI, ARTICHOKE, FENNEL, PARSLEY

1 stalk of broccoli
2 Jerusalem artichokes, cut into pieces
¼ head of fennel
3 sprigs of parsley

After thoroughly scrubbing all produce, put ingredients through a juicer.

GRAPEFRUIT, LEMON, PAPAYA

1 grapefruit
1 lemon
1 large piece of papaya

After thoroughly scrubbing all produce, put ingredients through a juicer.

CARROT, CELERY, GARLIC, PARSLEY

2 carrots
2 celery stalks
1 garlic clove
3 sprigs of parsley

After thoroughly scrubbing all produce, put ingredients through a juicer.

Grapefruit in a bowl

Carrot, Celery, Garlic, Parsley

SWEET DREAMS JUICE FOR SLEEP

2 large oranges, peeled
½ lemon, peeled
½ bunch organic watercress
8 stalks celery
½ head romaine lettuce

After thoroughly scrubbing all produce, put ingredients through a juicer.

ULTIMATE SLEEPER

1 cup cherries (pitted)
1½ cucumbers
1 banana
1 cup spinach
½ avocado

First, juice the cherries and cucumber, then blend with the banana, spinach, and avocado.

INSOMNIA SOOTHER

½ cabbage
1 large zucchini
½-inch piece ginger
3 cups broccoli florets
1 large head of green lettuce
6 medium-sized carrots
1 apple
1 pear

Wash and juice all ingredients. Makes three glasses of a strong mixture; drink one before dinner, one after—and the third only if you're still tossing and turning.

Ingredients for Ultimate Sleeper

Ultimate Sleeper

CARROT, CELERY, GINGER

4–5 large carrots, washed and scrubbed

1–2 celery stalks, washed

1 inch ginger, peeled

After thoroughly scrubbing all produce, put ingredients through a juicer.

TROPIKALE EASE

½ pineapple

3-4 kale leaves

1 stalk celery

¼ lemon

½ cucumber

½ inch ginger

After thoroughly scrubbing all produce, put ingredients through a juicer.

CLEAR SKIES

4 kale leaves

2 handfuls of spinach

3 celery stalks with leaves

¼ inch ginger

1 cucumber (peeled if not organic)

2 Fuji apples

After thoroughly scrubbing all produce, put ingredients through a juicer.

CARROT SPINACH

5 bunches of spinach

4 carrots

After thoroughly washing all produce, put ingredients through a juicer.

MIGRAINE SOOTHER

16 oz filtered water or coconut water

1 cup pineapple

1 cup kale (3-4 leaves)

1 stalk celery

½ lemon, juiced

1 cup cucumber (about ½ large cucumber)

½ inch ginger

1½ cups ice

After thoroughly scrubbing all produce, put ingredients in a blender and process until smooth.

Pineapple

Carrot, Celery, Ginger

Great Green Hair Regime

HAIR-ENHANCING JUICE

1 cup sprouts
1 cabbage leaf or 2 brussel sprouts
1 cup broccoli florets
2 medium carrots
2 slices red onion
1 medium beet with greens
½–1 clove garlic (optional)
2 slices of watermelon
2 apples.

After thoroughly scrubbing all produce, put ingredients through a juicer.

HAIR GROWTH TONIC

5 carrots
2 apples
½ cup alfalfa sprouts
handful of dark green kale

After thoroughly washing all produce, put ingredients through a juicer.

HAIR REPAIR JUICE

2 oz wheatgrass
½ handful of parsley
1 handful cilantro
4 carrots, cleaned of greens and skin
1 stalk celery
½ cup chopped fennel
½ apple, seeded

After washing all produce, put ingredients through a juicer.

HAPPY HAIR REGIME

3 large broccoli florets
2-3 green apples, seeded
handful of spinach
1 lime, peeled

After thoroughly washing all produce, put ingredients through a juicer.

HEALTHY HAIR

handful of parsley
handful of spinach
4-5 carrots, greens removed
2 stalks of celery

After thoroughly washing all produce, put ingredients through a juicer.

Healthy Hair

CARROT APPLE

1 carrot
2 green apples
1 bunch of spinach
3–4 leaves kale
¼ lemon slice

After thoroughly scrubbing all produce, put ingredients through a juicer.

GREEN THERAPY

2 carrots
1 bunch of spinach
1 cup broccoli
1 orange bell pepper
¼ lemon slice
1 inch ginger

After thoroughly scrubbing all produce, put ingredients through a juicer.

GINGER & VEGGIES

2 carrots
1 medium beet
1 bell pepper
¼ lemon slice

After thoroughly scrubbing all produce, put ingredients through a juicer.

JACK & JILL

3 carrots
½ small pumpkin
2 oranges

After thoroughly scrubbing all produce, put ingredients through a juicer.

CITRUS RELIEF

1 grapefruit
3 oranges
¼ lemon slice

Use a citrus juicer for this one, then mix the juices in a glass.

WHEATGRASS & LEMON JUICE

1 oz wheatgrass juice
a squeeze of lemon juice

Don't use a juicer for this one—you can buy or make fresh wheatgrass juice, and just squeeze the lemon into the glass.

Lemons

Citrus Relief

GREEN RELIEF

¾ cucumber
half an avocado
handful of watercress
sprig of parsley

Remove the stone from the avocado and scoop the flesh into the blender. Either juice the cucumber and watercress and add the juices to a blender with the avocado, or put all the ingredients in the blender and whiz to a smooth consistency.

MELON YELLOW

half a yellow melon

Cut the rind away from the flesh. Add flesh (and seeds) to juicer and enjoy.

JUICE BLEND

¼ small pineapple
½ stalk celery
¼ cucumber
1 handful of spinach leaves
1 small piece of peeled lime
2 apples
¼ ripe avocado
ice

Juice the pineapple, celery, cucumber, spinach, lime, and apples. Place the ripe avocado flesh in a blender with the ice and juice mixture. Blend until smooth.

Fresh honeydew melon

Melon Yellow

GINGER SWEET POTATO

1 sweet potato, peeled
1 large carrot, end removed
1 large slice pineapple, peeled, cored, about ½ cup fruit
¼ inch slice of ginger root, peeled

After thoroughly scrubbing all produce, put ingredients through a juicer.

KALE CLEAR

1 cup kale
1 cucumber
2 apples
½ bunch parsley
3 carrots

After thoroughly washing all produce, put ingredients through a juicer.

COCONUT CLEANSER

½ cantaloupe
glass of coconut water
½ cucumber

Peel and juice the cantaloupe, then juice the cucumber and mix with the coconut water.

AU REVOIR COFFEE

6 medium carrots
2 cloves garlic
1 handful of parsley

After thoroughly washing all produce, put ingredients through a juicer.

ONION & CARROT

4 medium carrots
½ medium onion
1 handful of parsley

After thoroughly scrubbing all produce, put ingredients through a juicer.

Onion & Carrot

Kale Clear

APPLE, ORANGE & GUAVA

2 cups apple juice
2 cups orange juice
2 cups guava nectar

After thoroughly scrubbing all produce, put ingredients through a juicer.

BLUEBERRIES, WATERMELON & CRANBERRIES

1½ cups of blueberries
2 cups watermelon, deseeded
½ cup cranberries
½ lemon, peeled

After thoroughly scrubbing all produce, put ingredients through a juicer.

GRAPEFRUIT, ORANGE & LEMON

5 grapefruits
2–3 oranges
½–1 lemon

After thoroughly scrubbing all produce, put ingredients through a juicer.

Slice of lemon

Grapefruit, Orange & Lemon

CARROT-PARSLEY

3 carrots
4 broccoli florets
handful of parsley

After washing all produce, roughly chop the carrots and break the broccoli into chunks. Reserve a sprig of parsley for decoration. Juice the carrots and broccoli separately, and combine the juices in a glass. Garnish with a sprig of parsley.

AVOCADO-TOMATO

½ avocado
4 medium tomatoes
2 sprigs of cilantro

Remove the stone from the avocado and scoop out the flesh. Combine the ingredients in a blender (avocados do not juice well). Garnish with a sprig of cilantro.

BLACKCURRANT ORANGE

2 oranges
5 oz blackcurrants

Peel the oranges and divide them into segments to fit in the feed tube. Rinse the blackcurrants and remove the stems. Juice each ingredient separately and combine the juices in a glass.

APPLE-GRAPE

5 oz grapes
5 oz blackcurrants
1 apple

After washing all produce, put ingredients through a juicer.

STRAWBERRY-BLACKCURRANT

5 oz blackcurrants
5 oz strawberries

Rinse the blackcurrants and remove the stems. Rinse and hull the strawberries. Juice each ingredient and combine the juices in a glass.

Washed grapes

Blackcurrant Orange

A to Z
JUICES

HAVE A FAVORITE FRUIT OR VEGETABLE? FIND IT HERE
(ORGANIZED BY FRUITS, THEN VEGETABLES, AND,
FINALLY, WHEATGRASS), AND TRY SOME OF THE JUICE
CONCOCTIONS THAT ARE SUGGESTED IN THIS SECTION.
BUT THESE ARE ONLY TO GIVE YOU AN IDEA OF WHAT
TO COMBINE AND HOW—NOW, CREATE YOUR OWN
SIGNATURE JUICES!

APPLE-CARROT JUICE

1 apple
1 carrot
1 stalk of celery

Wash the apple and the vegetables. Core the apple. Cut into pieces to fit the juicer.

WATERAPPLE

2 apples, cored
3 slices of watermelon, rind removed

After thoroughly scrubbing all produce, put ingredients through a juicer.

APPLE-STRAWBERRY NECTAR

2 cups fresh sliced strawberries
¼ cup unsweetened apple juice, or to taste
2 tbsp water, or as needed (optional)

After thoroughly washing all produce, put ingredients through a juicer.

APPLE, CARROT & TANGERINE

8 large carrots
1 Braeburn apple
1 Minneola tangerine

After thoroughly scrubbing all produce, put ingredients through a juicer.

APPLE CELERY

4 green apples
celery stalks (3–12 depending on the desired intensity of the celery taste)

After thoroughly scrubbing all produce, put ingredients through a juicer.

Waterapple

Apple, Carrot & Tangerine

BLUEBERRY CUCUMBER JUICE

1 cup blueberries
1 cucumber
½ lemon, rind removed
2 apples

After thoroughly washing all produce, put ingredients through a juicer.

BLUEBERRY GINGER JUICE

¼ pineapple
1 cup blueberries
¼–½ inch ginger

After thoroughly washing all produce, put ingredients through a juicer.

BLACKBERRY GRAPE

2 cups blackberries
2 cups black or purple grapes
2-inch piece of ginger

After thoroughly washing all produce, put ingredients through a juicer.

BLUEBERRY & BASIL LEMONADE

½ cup fresh lemon juice (about 3 lemons)
2 cups fresh blueberries
¼ cup fresh torn basil leaves
6 tbsp granulated sugar
4 cups water

Pour lemon juice into a pitcher. Add blueberries, basil, and sugar to the pitcher and muddle. Add water and allow to stand for 30 minutes. Pour through a fine mesh sieve into a bowl; discard the solids. Return mixture to the pitcher. Serve chilled over ice.

BLACKBERRY-KIWI JUICE

1 cup blackberries
1 kiwi (2 inches dia.)
1 medium pear
30 leaves peppermint
¼ pineapple, peeled and cored

After thoroughly washing all produce, put ingredients through a juicer.

Grapes and blackberries

Blackberry Grape

RASPBERRY, CARROT, PEAR & CUCUMBER

4 or 5 carrots
1 pear (green Anjou)
2 large handfuls of organic raspberries
1 cucumber

After thoroughly washing all produce, put ingredients through a juicer.

BERRY BLITZ

2 large handfuls of raspberries
1 handful of blackcurrants
1 handful of blueberries

After thoroughly washing all produce, put ingredients through a juicer.

RASPBERRY SENSATION

2 large handfuls of raspberries
1 apple
½ pineapple

After thoroughly washing all produce, put ingredients through a juicer.

CRANBERRY, POMEGRANATE & KALE JUICE

4–6 large leaves kale
1 cup pomegranate arils (from one large ripe pomegranate)
1 cup fresh or frozen cranberries (if frozen, thaw before juicing)
1 pear, cored
1 inch fresh ginger, peeled
6–12 leaves of fresh mint (optional)
stevia, to taste

After thoroughly scrubbing all produce, put ingredients through a juicer.

FRESH STRAWBERRIES WITH GINGER, CUCUMBER, SPINACH & APPLE

10–12 strawberries
1 inch fresh ginger
1 small cucumber
3 handfuls of fresh spinach (approximately 4 cups)
3 apples
½ lemon

After thoroughly washing all produce, put ingredients through a juicer.

BERRY BLAST

1 pound cranberries
2 pounds raspberries
2 oranges, peeled

Wash the cranberries and raspberries. Remove the stems and any other debris from the cranberries. Juice the berries first, and save the pulp for numerous other fruit toppings. Next, juice up the oranges. Mix the two together and serve over crushed ice.

STRAWBERRY LIME

3 cups fresh organic strawberries, stems removed and halved
1 apple
1 lime

After thoroughly scrubbing all produce, put ingredients through a juicer.

Raspberries in a bowl

Raspberry, Carrot, Pear & Cucumber

CITRUS BERRY JUICE

2 grapefruits
1 handful of blackberries
1 handful of blackcurrants

After thoroughly washing all produce, put ingredients through a juicer.

GRAPEFRUIT, APPLE & BEET JUICE

3 beets, thoroughly washed and peeled
1 whole grapefruit peeled
1 organic Fuji apple
3–4 organic carrots

After thoroughly scrubbing all produce, put ingredients through a juicer.

GRAPEFRUIT, LEMON & PINEAPPLE

1 grapefruit, peeled, halved, cut into wedges, seeds removed
½ ripe pineapple, peeled, cut lengthwise into quarters
1 lemon, peeled, halved, cut into wedges, seeds removed

After thoroughly scrubbing all produce, put ingredients through a juicer.

MINTY ORANGE JUICE

2 oranges, peeled
½ pink grapefruit, peeled
2 carrots
2 celery stalks
⅓ bunch of mint

After thoroughly scrubbing all produce, put ingredients through a juicer.

CITRUS CUCUMBER REVIVER

½ cucumber
2 oranges, peeled
1 lemon, peeled

After thoroughly scrubbing all produce, put ingredients through a juicer.

GRAPEFRUIT, CARROT & GINGER JUICE

2 chopped grapefruits (peel and pith removed)
5 chopped carrots
1 inch fresh ginger, peeled and chopped

After thoroughly scrubbing all produce, put ingredients through a juicer.

WATERMELON ORANGE JUICE

4 to 5 cups chopped watermelon cubes, deseeded

1 medium or large sized orange, juiced or ¾–1 cup orange juice

4–5 fresh mint leaves (optional)

organic unrefined cane sugar

a few fresh mint leaves for garnishing

ice cubes (optional)

Peel and chop the orange and extract the juice, using a juicer. Blend the watermelon, mint leaves, and sugar in a blender. Pour the watermelon juice in a jar or bowl. Add the orange juice to the watermelon juice. Stir well and serve immediately, with or without ice cubes, garnished with mint leaves.

Oranges

Minty Orange Juice

PAPAYA, MANGO & ORANGE JUICE

These three fruits can be combined in any combination and blended to your desired consistency.

After thoroughly scrubbing all produce, put ingredients through a juicer.

LIME, PAPAYA & MANGO JUICE

1 mango
½ standard papaya
2 cups of orange and mango juice
1 tbsp lime juice (the juice of ½ small lime)

After thoroughly scrubbing all produce, put ingredients through a juicer.

MANGO, ORANGE & BELL PEPPER JUICE

1 mango
2 orange bell peppers, seeded
1 naval orange, peeled
4 carrots
1 large handful of fresh pineapple chunks
1 lemon, peeled

After thoroughly scrubbing all produce, put ingredients through a juicer.

SUMMER MANGO JUICE

1 mango
1 cucumber
1 orange
5 carrots
handful of spinach
½ inch ginger

After thoroughly washing all produce, put ingredients through a juicer.

MANGO-JALPEÑO JUICE

1 mango
½ cucumber
¼ yellow bell pepper
½ jalapeño pepper
2 green onions or scallions (Australian shallots)
¼ cup cilantro
½ lime

After thoroughly scrubbing all produce, put ingredients through a juicer.

To make the juice less spicy remove ribs and seeds from jalapeño pepper.

Ingredients for Summer Mango Juice

Summer Mango Juice

ROCKIN' MELON JUICE

½ cantaloupe
4–6 leaves rainbow chard
1 apple
1 handful of fresh mint leaves

After thoroughly scrubbing all produce, put ingredients through a juicer.

WATERMELON, BLUEBERRIES & CHARD JUICE

2½ cups watermelon
1 cup blueberries
6–8 leaves Swiss chard

After thoroughly washing all produce, put ingredients through a juicer.

WATERMELON-LIME JUICE

3 cups diced watermelon (seedless)
1 lime (peel removed)

After thoroughly scrubbing all produce, put ingredients through a juicer.

HEAVEN'S HONEYDEW

1 handful of spinach with stems
¼ honeydew, rind removed
1 cucumber
½ lemon, peeled

Peel the lemon or scrub thoroughly. Wash and chop the ingredients to fit through your juicer.

Substitutions:
Spinach: kale, dandelion leaves, lettuce, watercress, choy sum
Honeydew: cantaloupe, pineapple, apple
Cucumber: celery, zucchini, celeriac root
Lemon: lime, grapefruit, orange

APPLE, CANTALOUPE & HONEYDEW

2 apples
½ cantaloupe
½ honeydew
6–8 kale leaves
6–8 Swiss chard leaves

After thoroughly washing all produce, put ingredients through a juicer.

MELON & ORANGE

½ melon, without rind
1 carrot
4 oranges, peeled

After thoroughly scrubbing all produce, put ingredients through a juicer.

Ingredients for Melon & Orange

Melon & Orange

PINEAPPLE, BLUEBERRY & GINGER

¼ pineapple
1 cup blueberries
½ inch ginger

After thoroughly washing all produce, put ingredients through a juicer.

BLACK & BLUE PINEAPPLE

1 cup blackberries
3 sprigs fresh parsley
2 spears pineapple
½ cup blueberries
½ cup raspberries

After thoroughly washing all produce, put ingredients through a juicer.

ANISEED PINEAPPLE

½ pineapple
1½ handfuls of blackcurrants
½ fennel bulb

After thoroughly washing all produce, put ingredients through a juicer.

PEAR PINEAPPLE

2 pears
¼ large pineapple
½ inch ginger

After thoroughly scrubbing all produce, put ingredients through a juicer.

PINK PINEAPPLE JUICE

½ pineapple
1 handful of raspberries
1 handful of strawberries

After thoroughly washing all produce, put ingredients through a juicer.

Pear Pineapple

Pink Pineapple Juice

BEET, APPLE & BLACKBERRY

3 small beets
2–3 apples
8 oz blackberries
½ inch ginger

After thoroughly washing all produce, put ingredients through a juicer.

RED KALE

8 kale leaves
1 ruby grapefruit
2 oranges

After thoroughly washing all produce, put ingredients through a juicer.

RUBY RED

2 pink grapefruit
2 stalks celery
½ beet

After thoroughly scrubbing all produce, put ingredients through a juicer.

SPICY SWEET BEET JUICE

1 small beet (reduce to a quarter of a beet if you don't eat raw beets regularly)
1 small carrot, peeled
¼ yellow bell pepper
2 lemon wedges (add some rind if you like a little tartness)
jalapeño pepper and cilantro according to taste
2 large romaine lettuce leaves (optional)

After thoroughly scrubbing all produce, put ingredients through a juicer.

BEET BASE

1 small beet
2 carrots
2 apples
1 handful of kale

After thoroughly washing all produce, put ingredients through a juicer.

PEAR, APPLE & BEET

2 apples, scrubbed
1 pear, scrubbed
3 medium or 2 large beets
1 lemon, peeled
½ inch ginger

After thoroughly scrubbing all produce, put ingredients through a juicer.

Blackberry

Beet Base

Red Kale

CARROT, BEET & ORANGE

3 medium beets, trimmed

2 medium carrots, scrubbed or peeled

4 oranges, peeled

After thoroughly scrubbing all produce, put ingredients through a juicer.

CAPPLE MINT

1 Granny Smith green apple

1 Red Delicious apple

2 large carrots, with tops

1 inch ginger

¼ cup peppermint, fresh (or other fresh mint)

After thoroughly scrubbing all produce, put ingredients through a juicer.

CARROT DELIGHT

2 carrots

1½ apples

½ lemon, peeled

4 leaves romaine lettuce

5 strawberries

After thoroughly scrubbing all produce, put ingredients through a juicer.

Oranges and carrots

Carrot, Beet & Orange

SAVORY CELERY JUICE

2 tomatoes
6 stalks of celery
1 stem and crown of broccoli
1 red bell pepper
1 lemon
½ bunch of green kale
½ bunch of curly parsley
½ bunch of cilantro
½ cup fresh basil
1 small clove of garlic

After thoroughly washing all produce, put ingredients through a juicer.

VEGETABLE COCKTAIL

¾ pound fresh tomatoes
2 tbsp chopped celery
⅛ large onions, peeled
⅛ green bell pepper
⅛ medium beet
¼ carrot
⅛ clove garlic, peeled
½ tsp sugar
⅛ tsp black pepper
⅛ tsp prepared horseradish
¾ tsp lemon juice
1 cup and 3 tbsp water, or as needed
⅛ tsp Worcestershire sauce, or to taste
2½ tsp brown sugar
½ tsp salt, or to taste

After thoroughly washing all produce, put ingredients through a juicer.

FENNELTASTIC

2 small fennel bulbs
3 small apples
1 lemon, whole
8 leaves kale
¼ medium-sized green cabbage

After thoroughly washing all produce, put ingredients through a juicer.

CELERY WITH CARROTS & APPLE

3 carrots
½ cucumber
2 apples
2 celery sticks

After thoroughly scrubbing all produce, put ingredients through a juicer.

FENNEL FEST

2 large apples
½ lime peeled
2 cucumbers
4 stalks celery
1–2 large handfuls of fennel
1-inch piece of ginger

After thoroughly scrubbing all produce, put ingredients through a juicer.

ORANGE FENNEL

1 wedge purple cabbage
4 kale leaves
1 large cucumber
½ fennel bulb
2 oranges
1 apple

After thoroughly scrubbing all produce, put ingredients through a juicer.

Celery with Carrots & Apple

TOMATO-KALE WITH CELERY, HORSERADISH & SOY

1 tbsp prepared horseradish

1 tbsp soy sauce

½ cup plus 2 tbsp fresh tomato juice (from about 2 pints grape or cherry tomatoes)

¼ cup fresh kale juice (from about ½ pound kale)

2 tbsp fresh celery juice (from 4 stalks celery)

2 tbsp juice from 2 lemons

dash of hot sauce

Garnish: celery stalk

Mix horseradish and soy sauce in a glass. Add tomato juice and stir well until horseradish is well distributed. Add kale juice, celery juice, lemon juice, and hot sauce. Stir well. Serve with celery stalk garnish, over ice if desired.

PARSNIP, APPLE, MINT, LIME & KALE

1 cup freshly squeezed kale juice, from about 1½ pounds kale

½ cup parsnip juice, from about 4 peeled parsnips

½ cup fresh apple juice, from 4 large (or up to 8 small) green apples

4 tsp juice from 1 lime (more or less to taste)

¼ cup mint juice, from about 12 oz mint leaves (about 2 large bunches)

Garnish: mint sprig and lime wedge

After thoroughly scrubbing all produce, put ingredients through a juicer.

ULTIMATE GREEN DREAM

2 green apples

2 celery stalks

½ cucumber

3 leaves kale

¼ lemon, peeled

½-inch piece fresh ginger

After thoroughly scrubbing all produce, put ingredients through a juicer.

HAIL KING KALE

3 leaves of green kale

2 apples

2 slices of watermelon

¼ lemon, peeled

After thoroughly scrubbing all produce, put ingredients through a juicer.

CELERY KALE JUICE

3 apples

16–20 stalks of celery

2 handfuls of kale

1 chunk of ginger

1 lemon

After thoroughly scrubbing all produce, put ingredients through a juicer.

Sliced apples

Celery Kale Juice

PARSNAPPLE

3 parsnips
3 apples
½ lime
3 sprigs fresh mint

After thoroughly washing all produce, put ingredients through a juicer.

RUPERT THE PEAR

3 parsnips
3 pears
1 lime

After thoroughly scrubbing all produce, put ingredients through a juicer.

TRIATHLON

6 tomatoes
2 parsnips
2 stalks celery
1 small handful of fresh basil leaves

After thoroughly washing all produce, put ingredients through a juicer.

CITRUS FROOTJUICE

2 grapefruit
2-inch slice of sweet potato
1 parsnip
1 stalk celery

After thoroughly scrubbing all produce, put ingredients through a juicer.

MINTY PARSNAPPLE

3 apples
4 parsnips
1 lime
small bunch fresh mint

After thoroughly scrubbing all produce, put ingredients through a juicer.

Parsnapple

Triathlon

SPINACH & APPLE JUICE

1½ cups spinach

½ grapefruit, peeled, with pith removed

2 green apples, cut into eighths

1-inch piece peeled fresh ginger

2 large stalks celery

ice (optional)

After thoroughly washing all produce, put ingredients through a juicer.

SPINACH CARROT PINEAPPLE CILANTRO

a big handful of spinach (3 oz)

2 medium carrots

¼ pineapple

small bunch of cilantro (½ ounce; optional)

1 lime

1 drop liquid cayenne

After thoroughly washing all produce, put ingredients through a juicer.

SPINACH, BLUEBERRY, APPLE & LEMON

a small handful of spinach

1 pint of blueberries (10 oz)

1 Granny Smith apple, cored and cut into quarters

1 lemon, peeled

After thoroughly washing all produce, put ingredients through a juicer.

SPINACH CUCUMBER

2 cups packed spinach (4 oz)

1 cucumber

1 celery stalk

After thoroughly washing all produce, put ingredients through a juicer.

SPINACH LEMONADE

½ chopped lemon

2 cups baby spinach

1 chopped cucumber

2 cored and chopped sweet apples

After thoroughly washing all produce, put ingredients through a juicer.

HEALTHY JUICE

2 heads of broccoli

4 cups spinach, chard, or kale (or a mixture)

1 green bell pepper

2 Granny Smith apples

1 lime, peeled

After thoroughly washing all produce, put ingredients through a juicer.

Washed spinach in a bowl

Spinach Cucumber

VIRGIN MARY

6 tomatoes
2 red bell peppers
1 orange bell pepper
2 carrots
1 zucchini
large handful of fresh herbs (oregano, basil and parsley)
Himalayan salt to taste
1–2 tsp olive oil

Chop all ingredients. Juice. Add salt and oil, and stir.

Substitutions:

Tomato: extra red bell peppers

Orange bell pepper: yellow bell pepper, carrot, sweet potato, butternut squash, pumpkin

Carrot: sweet potato, butternut squash, pumpkin

Zucchini: celery

TOMATO & MANGO JUICE

1 tomato, medium sized
1 mango, cut into spears
¼ to ⅓ pineapple, cut into spears

After thoroughly scrubbing all produce, put ingredients through a juicer.

BRUSCHETTA

2 medium tomatoes
1–2 cloves garlic, peeled
25 fresh basil leaves

After thoroughly scrubbing all produce, put ingredients through a juicer.

Fresh garlic

Red bell peppers

Bruschetta

WHEATGRASS
JUICES

WHEATGRASS HAS BEEN TOUTED AS A CURE-ALL FOR A

MULTITUDE OF CONDITIONS. YOU CAN GROW YOUR OWN—

BY ALL ACCOUNTS IT'S A LOT OF FUN FOR THE ENTIRE

FAMILY—OR, IF YOU DON'T HAVE ROOM TO GROW IT OR

A WHEATGRASS JUICER, YOU CAN BUY IT IN OUNCE-SIZE

QUANTITIES TO ADD TO SMOOTHIES OR JUICES. BEFORE

YOU TURN UP YOUR NOSE AT USING SOMETHING THAT

ISN'T TOTALLY FRESH, THESE ACTUALLY WORK VERY

WELL AND KEEP ALL OF THE NUTRITIONAL BENEFITS OF

FRESHLY JUICED WHEATGRASS.

GREEN ORANGE

3 oranges
1 tbsp grated ginger
1 oz wheatgrass juice

After thoroughly scrubbing the oranges, put ingredients through a juicer. Garnish with mint leaves.

APPLE CARROT DELIGHT

3 carrots
2 apples
1 oz wheatgrass juice
1-inch piece of ginger (optional)

After thoroughly scrubbing all produce, put ingredients through a juicer.

SIMPLE APPLEGRASS

1 oz wheatgrass juice
2 medium apples

After thoroughly scrubbing the apples, put ingredients through a juicer.

CARROT SPECIAL

3 carrots
½ beet
2 celery sticks
½ lemon
1 oz wheatgrass juice
small handful of parsley and/or mint

After thoroughly scrubbing all produce, put ingredients through a juicer.

MINTY APPLES

2 apples
small handful of fresh mint
1 oz wheatgrass juice

After thoroughly scrubbing the apples, put ingredients through a juicer.

WHEATGRASS REVIVER

A great refreshing summer combination that disguises the taste of wheatgrass.
1 oz wheatgrass juice
½ watermelon (enough for 1 glass)

After thoroughly scrubbing the watermelon, put ingredients through a juicer.

Celery

Minty Apples

FRESH JUICY CLEANSER

1 oz wheatgrass
2 carrots
2 apples
1 celery stalk
1 thin slice of beet
¼ medium size cucumber
½ inch ginger

After thoroughly scrubbing all produce, put ingredients through a juicer.

PINEAPPLE WHEATGRASS

1 cup of roughly chopped wheatgrass
6½ cups roughly chopped pineapple
6 to 8 sprigs of mint
1 cup crushed ice

After thoroughly scrubbing the pineapple, blend all ingredients until smooth.

GREEN DRINK

3 stalks celery
2 medium cucumbers
5 fresh spinach leaves
½ cup fresh parsley
2 oz fresh wheatgrass
water as needed

Cut celery and cucumber into chunks small enough to fit through your juicer. Juice and then dilute with pure spring water for texture and taste.

Ingredients for Green Drink

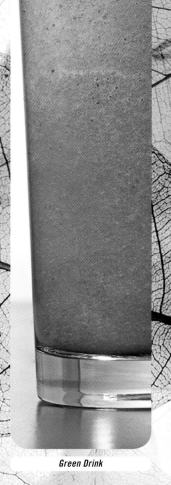

Green Drink

THE SUNBLAST

1 oz fresh organic wheatgrass juice
6 oz fresh carrot juice

Mix juices together and drink while fresh.

LEMON GRASS

6 oz lemonade
2 oz fresh organic wheatgrass juice

After thoroughly scrubbing all produce, put ingredients through a juicer.

Lemon Grass

GINGER WHEATGRASS JUICE

1 bunch of wheatgrass (about a handful)
1 lemon
3 large apples
3 carrots
2-inch piece of ginger

Send all ingredients through your juicer. If using a juice press, blend ingredients in a blender with a few inches of water. Send the mixture through the juice press. Serve and enjoy! Refrigerate any leftover ginger lemonade.

SIMPLY WHEATGRASS

3 celery stalks
4 large spinach leaves
½ cup parsley
2–3 inch round of wheatgrass
¼ cup water (optional)

Wash greens thoroughly, cut up celery and juice. Dilute with water if desired

TROPICAL WHEATGRASS

2 kiwi
1 guava or papaya
1 cup pineapple
5 strawberries
3–4 inch round of wheatgrass

After thoroughly washing all produce, put ingredients through a juicer.

PINEAPPLE & PAPAYA GRASS

2 cups fresh pineapple
1 papaya
2–3 inch round of wheatgrass

After thoroughly scrubbing all produce, put ingredients through a juicer.

APPLE WHEATGRASS

1–2 apples
¼ cup water (optional)
2–3 inch round of wheatgrass

After thoroughly scrubbing all produce, put ingredients through a juicer.

CARROT WHEATGRASS

3 carrots
2–3 inch round of wheatgrass
¼ cup water (optional)

After thoroughly scrubbing all produce, put ingredients through a juicer.

Ingredients for Tropical Wheatgrass

Tropical Wheatgrass

VEGGIE POWER

2 large carrots
3 stalks celery
½ cup parsley
4 large spinach leaves
½ beet
½ cup alfalfa sprouts

After thoroughly scrubbing all produce, put ingredients through a juicer.

GINGER GRASS

1 inch fresh ginger
1 oz wheatgrass juice
½ lemon
2½ cups water

After thoroughly washing all produce, put ingredients through a juicer.

BLUEBERRY SURPRISE

15–25 blueberries
1 oz wheatgrass juice

After thoroughly scrubbing all produce, put ingredients through a juicer.

GREEN GRASS

1 oz wheatgrass
2 stalks celery
handful of parsley

After thoroughly washing all produce, put ingredients through a juicer.

MINTY MADAM

handful of mint leaves
1 oz fresh wheatgrass juice

After thoroughly washing all produce, put ingredients through a juicer.

GRAPES & GRASS

7–10 red grapes
1 oz wheatgrass juice

After thoroughly washing all produce, put ingredients through a juicer.

Blueberry Surprise

Grapes & Grass

FRUITY
& SOY SMOOTHIES

SMOOTHIES OFFER A TOTALLY DIFFERENT EXPERIENCE FROM JUICES, WITH THEIR SLUSHY OR CREAMY CONSISTENCY. SMOOTHIES ALSO HAVE THE POTENTIAL TO BE FAR MORE CALORIC THAN JUICES, ALTHOUGH THEY DON'T HAVE TO BE. FRUIT- AND VEGGIE-BASED SMOOTHIES CAN BE THE FOUNDATION OF A LIFE-CHANGING WEIGHT-LOSS REGIMEN. SMOOTHIES FOR DESSERT OR AFTER-DINNER COFFEE ARE NOTHING LESS THAN DECADENT.

FRUITY AND CREAMY

THE HEALTHY WAY TO INDULGE

While juices may win the prize for offering nutrition-packed combos of fruits and veggies that are unquestionably healthy, the process of juicing extracts the pulp—and, therefore, most of the dietary fiber that would be provided by the constituents—leaving a product that is high in natural sugars but low in fiber. Smoothies, on the other hand, keep their fiber because the entire fruit or vegetable is tossed into the blender and pulverized together rather than being pulped.

Most smoothies have a creamy or slushy consistency that is provided by soft fruits or vegetables that would merely clog up a juicer, such as bananas or avocados, or by juices, yogurt, tofu, or milk. But each of these foods provide important nutrients that are necessary for proper functioning, such as omega-3 oils from avocados or probiotics from yogurt. So, any time you want to reach for a cool, thick drink, satisfy your craving instead with a healthy—and totally delicious—fruit shake.

Avocado smoothie

Pear and berry smoothie

Banana Berry Smoothie

BANANA SMOOTHIE

½ cup pineapple juice
1½ bananas, sliced
1½ tsp honey

Put all of the ingredients into a blender and blend until smooth.

BANANA APPLE SMOOTHIE

1 frozen banana, peeled and chopped
½ cup orange juice
1 Gala apple, peeled, cored, and chopped
¼ cup milk

Wash all produce, then put all of the ingredients into a blender and blend until smooth.

BANANA HONEY SMOOTHIE

1 cup freshly squeezed orange juice (about 6 oranges)
2 tbsp raw honey
1 tbsp freshly squeezed lemon juice
2 tsp finely grated fresh ginger
2 ripe bananas

Put all of the ingredients into a blender and blend until smooth.

BANANA STRAWBERRY SMOOTHIE

1 banana, broken into chunks
1 tsp banana extract
¾ cup milk
8 oz strawberry yogurt
2 tsp white sugar

Put all of the ingredients into a blender and blend until smooth.

BUTTERMILK & BANANA SMOOTHIE

1 cup low-fat buttermilk
2 ripe bananas, cut into 2-inch-thick rounds
11 dried pitted dates
1 tsp honey
pinch of salt
1 cup ice

Put all of the ingredients into a blender and blend until smooth.

BANANA BERRY SMOOTHIE

1 banana
1 cup frozen raspberries
¾ cup orange juice
¼ cup vanilla yogurt

Put all of the ingredients into a blender and blend until smooth.

RASPBERRY-BLACKBERRY SMOOTHIE

1 banana
½ cup blackberries
1 cup raspberries
6 oz vanilla yogurt
1 tbsp honey
4 ice cubes

Wash all produce, then put all of the ingredients into a blender and blend until smooth.

BERRY YOGURT SMOOTHIE

1 handful of blueberries
1 handful of blackcurrants
5 tbsp natural yogurt
6 tbsp apple juice

Wash all produce, then put all of the ingredients into a blender and blend until smooth.

BLACKBERRY CINNAMON SMOOTHIE

1½ cups frozen blackberries
½ cup low-fat plain yogurt
½ cup low-fat buttermilk
1 tbsp honey
⅛ tsp ground cinnamon

Wash all produce, then put all of the ingredients into a blender and blend until smooth.

BERRY & TOFU SMOOTHIE

1 lb fresh strawberries, cleaned and hulled
2 cups blueberries
9 oz tofu
½ tsp ground ginger
2 pinches of red pepper flakes
¼ tsp rum extract
1 tbsp honey
1 tsp lemon juice
½ cup ice

Wash all produce, then put all of the ingredients into a blender and blend until smooth.

BLACKBERRY YOGURT SMOOTHIE

1 cup fresh blackberries
½ frozen banana
6 oz low-fat Greek yogurt
4 cubes of ice
½–¾ cup unsweetened almond milk or other type of milk

Wash all produce, then put all of the ingredients into a blender and blend until smooth.

BLUEBERRY BREAKFAST SMOOTHIE

1 cup blueberries
½ cup low-fat vanilla yogurt
½ cup skim milk
2 tbsp honey
5 ice cubes

Wash all produce, then put all of the ingredients into a blender and blend until smooth.

Blackberry Yogurt Smoothie

Fresh blackberries

APPLE, CARROT & GINGER SMOOTHIE

¾ cup ice cubes

2 green apples, cored and quartered

2 medium carrots, ends trimmed, cut into one-inch lengths

½–1 inch ginger

½ navel orange, peel and pith removed

½ small banana, peeled

1 tbsp golden flax seed meal (optional)

½–1 cup water (depending on preferred consistency)

Wash all produce, then put all of the ingredients into a blender and blend until smooth.

APPLE AVOCADO SMOOTHIE

1 Granny Smith apple, cored, skin on

½ ripe Hass avocado

½ cup apple juice

½ cup ice

3 sprigs mint leaves

1 tsp freshly squeezed lime juice

Wash all produce, then put all of the ingredients into a blender and blend until smooth.

ACORN SQUASH-APPLE SMOOTHIE

1 small acorn squash

1 large apple

2 cups apple juice

1½ tsp fresh ginger, grated

Wash the squash, cut it in half, and scoop out the seeds. Place it, cut side down, in a dish with about 1/2 an inch of water and microwave it for about 10 minutes. Let it cool in the refrigerator. Peel the apple, core it, chop it, and place it into a blender. Scoop out the squash from the skin and add it into the blender. Add the apple juice and the ginger, and puree.

CARROT, ORANGE & APPLE SMOOTHIE

½ cup cold water

1 orange, quartered, including white part of peel

½ apple, seeded, halved

½ inch slice of pineapple, core included

1 medium carrot

1 cup ice cubes

Wash apple, then put all of the ingredients into a blender and blend until smooth.

BIG APPLE SMOOTHIE

2 large scoops of fat-free vanilla yogurt

¼ cup of vanilla soy milk

½ cup of apple juice

½ tsp pure vanilla extract

½ tbsp pure maple syrup

¼ tsp of ground cinnamon

pinch of ground nutmeg

Put all of the ingredients into a blender and blend until smooth.

APPLE YOGURT WITH CARDAMOM

½ cup chopped apple, cored but not peeled

½ cup low-fat plain yogurt

1 tbsp honey

pinch of ground cardamom

½ cup unsweetened apple juice

½ banana

2–3 ice cubes

Wash apple, then put all of the ingredients into a blender and blend until smooth.

Apple, Carrot & Ginger Smoothie

Green cardamom

Apple Yogurt with Cardamom

Mango-Papaya Smoothie

MANGO, PEACH, STRAWBERRY SMOOTHIE

2 small peaches
1 mango
6 frozen strawberries
1 frozen banana
½ cup almond milk
¾ cup vanilla yogurt
6 ice cubes

Wash all produce, then put all of the ingredients into a blender and blend until smooth.

MANGO-LIME SMOOTHIE

2 cups ripe mango chunks
2–3 tbsp fresh lime juice
2 cups unsweetened coconut water
pinch of cayenne powder

Wash all produce, then put all of the ingredients into a blender and blend until smooth.

MANGO-PAPAYA SMOOTHIE

1¼ cups almond milk
½ cup coconut water (not coconut milk)
1 cup papaya, peeled and cubed
1 cup mango, peeled and cubed
½ cup ice

Wash all produce, then put all of the ingredients into a blender and blend until smooth.

CARROT-MANGO SMOOTHIE

1 mango, chopped
2 medium carrots, peeled and finely grated
dash freshly grated nutmeg
1 cup water
2 tbsp lime juice
½ cup ice cubes

Wash all produce, then put all of the ingredients into a blender and blend until smooth.

MANGO, PAPAYA, PINEAPPLE SMOOTHIE

1 cup frozen mango
1 cup frozen pineapple
1 cup peeled, seeded, and diced papaya
½ cup low-fat Greek yogurt
½–¾ cup whole or skim milk, or orange juice

Wash all produce, then put all of the ingredients into a blender and blend until smooth.

MANGO-PINEAPPLE SMOOTHIE

1 cup frozen pineapple
1 cup frozen mango pieces
1 cup vanilla yogurt
⅓ cup milk (or more if needed)
2 tsp sugar
2 ice cubes, if needed

Put all of the ingredients into a blender and blend until smooth.

Orange-Berry Smoothie

ORANGE-BERRY SMOOTHIE

2 navel oranges, peel and pith removed, cut into chunks

1 cup frozen blueberries

1 cup frozen raspberries

Wash all produce, then put all of the ingredients into a blender and blend until smooth.

MAGNIFICENT STRAWBERRY-ORANGE SMOOTHIE

½ cup chopped fresh strawberries

½ cup orange juice

5 cubes ice

1½ tsp sugar

Wash strawberries, then put all of the ingredients into a blender and blend until smooth.

STRAWBERRY, ORANGE, COCONUT SMOOTHIE

2½ cups hulled strawberries

1 peeled orange

½ cup coconut milk

4 ice cubes (optional)

Wash all produce, then put all of the ingredients into a blender and blend until smooth.

GOLDEN HONEY SMOOTHIE

2 cups freshly squeezed orange juice (about 6 oranges)

¼ cup plus 1 tbsp raw honey

1 tbsp freshly squeezed lemon juice

2 tsp finely grated fresh ginger

2 ripe bananas

Put all of the ingredients into a blender and blend until smooth.

BLOOD ORANGE, BANANA, BERRY SMOOTHIE

2 medium bananas

1 blood orange

½ cup frozen blueberries

½ cup frozen blackberries

1 cup açaí berry juice

Put all of the ingredients into a blender and blend until smooth.

CRANBERRY-ORANGE POWER SMOOTHIE

1 cup cranberry juice

1 large banana

1 medium orange, peeled and segmented

½ cup strawberries, hulled

¼ cup raspberry sherbet

1 cup ice cubes

¼ cup whey protein powder

Wash all produce, then put all of the ingredients into a blender and blend until smooth.

ALMOND-ORANGE SMOOTHIE

1 cup vanilla-flavored almond beverage
½ cup orange juice
juice from one lemon
juice from one lime
handful of ice
1 tbsp honey

Put all of the ingredients into a blender and blend until smooth.

GRAPEFRUIT SURPRISE

2 red grapefruits
8 large strawberries
2 ripe bananas
8 oz strawberry-banana yogurt
2 tbsp honey
1 cup crushed ice

Juice grapefruit; measure 1⅓ cups juice. Add strawberries. Cut bananas into chunks. Combine all the ingredients in a blender and whirl until smooth.

GRAPEFRUIT-CARROT-GINGER SMOOTHIE

2 chopped grapefruits (peel and pith removed)
5 chopped carrots
1 inch fresh ginger, peeled and chopped

Press grapefruits, carrots, and ginger through a juice extractor. Stir and serve immediately.

GRAPEFRUIT MANGO SMOOTHIE

fresh-squeezed juice from 3 grapefruits
1 mango, cubed
2 frozen bananas

Wash all produce, then put all of the ingredients into a blender and blend until smooth.

C-VIT SMOOTHIE

1 large pink grapefruit, peeled, seeded, and cut into chunks
½ cup crushed pineapple, canned or fresh
½ cup fresh strawberries
½ cup non-fat Greek yogurt
½ cup ice

Wash all produce, then put all of the ingredients into a blender and blend until smooth.

SWEET GRAPEFRUIT, ORANGE & BANANA SMOOTHIE

1 grapefruit
1 large orange
1 banana

Give a squeeze to both the grapefruit and orange when you add them to your blender so that you have some free liquid to help blend. If you have difficulty blending this smoothie in your blender, add a little bit of water or extra squeezed orange juice.

Grapefruit Surprise

PAPAYA GINGER SMOOTHIE

2½ cups papaya (Solo or Mexican) chunks
1 cup ice cubes
⅔ cup nonfat plain yogurt
1 tbsp finely chopped peeled fresh ginger
1 tbsp honey
juice of 2 lemons
16 fresh mint leaves, plus 4 sprigs for garnish

Refrigerate papaya until very cold, at least 1 hour or overnight. Blend papaya, ice, yogurt, ginger, honey, and lemon juice in a blender. Add up to ¼ cup water, 1 tablespoon at a time, until mixture is smooth and thinned to desired consistency. Blend in mint leaves. Garnish with mint sprigs

CARIBBEAN DREAM

6 oz light rum
½ cup papaya
½ cup mango
1 orange
1 inch ginger
2 tbsp fine cut dried unsweetened coconut
¼ tsp nutmeg
2 tbsp sugar or sugar substitute
1¼ cups cream or milk

Put all the ingredients into a blender or food processor and whiz on pulse and then high until smooth.

STRAWBERRY PAPAYA PASSION SMOOTHIE

½ cup plain fat-free yogurt
½ cup nonfat milk
¾ cup chopped papaya, chilled
½ cup strawberry, chilled
1 tbsp honey
½ cup small ice cubes or crushed ice

In blender, combine yogurt and milk; add papaya, strawberries and honey. Add ice cubes. Cover and blend until nearly smooth.

PAPAYA SMOOTHIE

1 small papaya, peeled, seeded, and diced
1 banana, sliced
½ cup sliced strawberries
pineapple wedges and/or maraschino cherries, for garnish

Combine the papaya, banana, strawberries and about 15 ice cubes in a blender and puree until smooth. Pour into 2-ounce shot glasses and garnish with pineapple and/or cherries.

PAPAYA PEACH NECTAR SMOOTHIE

1 medium, ripe papaya, peeled and seeded
¾ cup peach nectar
juice of 1 lime (about 2 tbsp)
1 cup ice

Add all the ingredients to the blender. Pulse intermittently until it begins to swirl. Blend on high until smooth, about 20 seconds.

PAPAYA BERRY SMOOTHIE

1 cup papaya, peeled and seeded
1 cup frozen mixed berries
½ cup skim milk or soymilk
1 tbsp honey (optional)

Put all of the ingredients into a blender and blend until smooth.

Caribbean Dream

POMEGRANATE BERRY

½ cup chilled pomegranate juice
½ cup vanilla low-fat yogurt
1 cup frozen mixed berries

Put all of the ingredients into a blender and blend until smooth.

PLUM YOGURT SMOOTHIE

1 cup vanilla yogurt
1 plum, pitted
½ banana
¼ cup almond milk
ice as needed

Put all of the ingredients into a blender and blend until smooth.

POMEGRANATE-BANANA SMOOTHIE

2 cups plain non-fat yogurt, well chilled
2 cups pure pomegranate juice (fresh squeezed or bottled fresh), well chilled
2 large bananas, thickly sliced crosswise

In a blender, combine the chilled nonfat yogurt with the pomegranate juice. Add the sliced bananas and puree.

PRICKLY PEAR-POMEGRANATE

1½ cups prickly pear, peeled and chopped
seeds from 1 pomegranate
¾ cup freshly squeezed orange juice
¼ cup cashew milk
¼ cup banana, chopped
1½ tsp fresh ginger, peeled and minced
2 cups crushed ice

Put all of the ingredients into a blender and blend until smooth.

VANILLA, PLUM & BUTTERMILK SMOOTHIE

2 cups sugar
1 vanilla bean, halved with scraped seeds reserved
5 plums, quartered, pitted
½ cup buttermilk
1½ cups small ice cubes

Put 4 cups water, sugar, and halved vanilla bean with scraped seeds into a large saucepan. Bring to a boil over medium-high heat, stirring until sugar has dissolved. Add plums. Reduce heat to medium-low, and simmer until plums are tender, about 15 minutes. Using a slotted spoon, transfer plums to a plate to cool completely; remove bean, and discard poaching liquid.

Puree cooled plums in a blender. Add buttermilk and small ice cubes; blend until smooth.

PLUM, RED GRAPE & ALMOND MILK

2½ small or 2 large plums, pitted and sliced (about ¾ cup sliced)
½ cup red grapes, rinsed
1 to 2 tsp rose geranium syrup
1 tbsp almond meal
⅛ tsp vanilla extract
¼ cup almond milk
3 to 4 ice cubes

Place all of the ingredients in a blender and blend until frothy, about one minute.

Pomegranate Berry

Pomegranate cut open showing seeds

Freshly picked plums

Plum Yogurt Smoothie

Pineapple, Coconut, Banana Smoothie

PINEAPPLE GINGER

1 cup fresh or frozen pineapple, cut into 1-inch pieces

1-inch piece fresh ginger, peeled and minced

½ cup low-fat plain yogurt

1 cup pineapple juice

⅛ tsp ground cinnamon

½ cup ice (if using fresh pineapple)

Put all of the ingredients into a blender and blend until smooth.

PINEAPPLE BERRY SMOOTHIE

½ cup mixed berries

½ cup water

½ cup ice

½ cup diced pineapple

1 banana

½ cup Greek yogurt

1 tbsp grated ginger

Put all of the ingredients into a blender and blend until smooth.

PINEAPPLE, COCONUT, BANANA SMOOTHIE

½ cup coconut milk

½ cup plain or vanilla yogurt

1 medium banana

1 cup chopped pineapple

¼ cup shredded coconut

1 tsp vanilla extract

¾ cup ice

1 tbsp honey

2 tbsp lime juice

Put all of the ingredients into a blender and blend until smooth.

PINEAPPLE & PASSION FRUIT SMOOTHIE

½ pineapple

2 bananas

2 passion fruits

8 tbsp pineapple juice

Put all of the ingredients into a blender and blend until smooth.

PINEAPPLE-POMEGRANATE SMOOTHIE

½ pineapple, chopped (including the core)

1½ cups pomegranate seeds

a few handfuls of ice

Put all of the ingredients into a blender and blend until smooth.

PLUM YOGURT SMOOTHIE

1 cup vanilla yogurt

1 plum, pitted

½ banana

¼ cup almond milk

ice as needed

Put all of the ingredients into a blender and blend until smooth.

PINK PINEAPPLE SMOOTHIE WITH GUAVA

½ pineapple
1 handful of strawberries
5 tbsp natural yogurt
8 tbsp guava juice

Put all of the ingredients into a blender and blend until smooth.

BLUE CRANBERRY SMOOTHIE

1 cup frozen blueberries
¼ cup frozen whole cranberries
½ cup vanilla nonfat yogurt
½ cup cranberry juice

Place the cranberry juice in the blender first, yogurt second, and frozen fruits last. Start on a slow speed until the blades are smoothly turning and then push to high for 30 seconds or so.

BERRY, BANANA, AGAVE SMOOTHIE

1 cup plain fat-free yogurt
⅓ cup fresh or frozen blueberries, thawed
2 tsp light-colored agave nectar
1 chilled sliced ripe banana

Put all of the ingredients into a blender and blend until smooth.

LEMON-MELON SMOOTHIE

1½ cups diced honeydew melon
½ cup nonfat lemon yogurt
1 cup frozen green grapes
1 tbsp chopped fresh mint
fresh lemon juice to taste (optional)

Combine the honeydew melon and lemon yogurt in a blender. Add the grapes and mint. Blend until smooth. Taste and add lemon juice if you like.

STRAWBERRY-GRAPEFRUIT SMOOTHIE

1 grapefruit, peeled, seeded, and chopped
2 cups hulled fresh or frozen strawberries
1 sweet apple (such as Honeycrisp or Pink Lady), cored and chopped
1 cup water
1-inch piece of fresh ginger, peeled and chopped

Wash all produce, then put all of the ingredients into a blender and blend until smooth.

STRAWBERRY-APPLE YOGURT

½ cup low-fat milk
½ cup strawberry, vanilla, or other fruit yogurt
2 tsp honey
1 cup frozen strawberries
1 apple, cored and peeled
2 tsp ground flax seeds

Put all of the ingredients into a blender and blend until smooth.

Strawberry-Apple Yogurt

Beet, Strawberry & Cranberry Smoothie

BEET, STRAWBERRY & CRANBERRY SMOOTHIE

¾ cup cranberry juice, chilled

¼ cup cranberries, fresh or frozen

1 small beet, steamed

⅓ cup frozen strawberries

2 tsp honey or other sweetener, to taste

⅔ cup ice cubes

Put all of the ingredients into a blender and blend until smooth.

GUAVA-CARROT WITH GINGER SMOOTHIE

½ cup guava, seeds removed

2 medium carrots, chopped

1 medium banana, peeled

2 medium peaches

1 tsp fresh ginger, grated

1 cup filtered water or coconut water

Put all of the ingredients into a blender and blend until smooth.

CLEMENTINE, BANANA & PINEAPPLE SMOOTHIE

8 clementines, segmented

½ cup fresh pineapple, cubed

1 banana, sliced

1 cup milk or plain yogurt

1 handful of ice cubes

Put all of the ingredients into a blender and blend until smooth.

BEET, CARROT & APPLE SMOOTHIE

2 beets, about 8 oz. total, peeled and cut into chunks

2 carrots, about 4 oz. total, peeled and cut into chunks

1 Granny Smith apple, cored and sliced

1 cup ice cubes

¾ cup sweetened cranberry juice

Put all of the ingredients into a blender and blend until smooth.

VANILLA, BLACKBERRY, OAT, ALMOND MILK SMOOTHIE

3 tbsp oats

1 cup blackberries

1 cup almond milk

1 banana, frozen

½ cup vanilla yogurt

1 tsp vanilla extract

In a blender, combine the almond milk and oats, and pulse a few times to pulverize the oats. Add the banana, blackberries, yogurt, and vanilla extract, and blend until smooth.

BERRY SMOOTHIE

1 cup coconut milk

1 cup blueberries

½ cup chopped mango

½ cup cooked, chopped beets

¼ avocado

1 tbsp fresh lemon juice (optional)

½ cup ice

Put all of the ingredients into a blender and blend until smooth.

SOY MILK SMOOTHIE

½ cup pineapple cubes
1 small banana
½ cup frozen raspberries
1 tbsp honey
¼ cup carrot juice
½ cup vanilla soy milk
½ cup freshly squeezed orange juice

Put all of the ingredients into a blender and blend until smooth.

WILD BLUEBERRY SMOOTHIE

1 cup frozen blueberries
1 cup vanilla soy milk
1 banana, frozen
3–4 dashes cayenne or 1 tsp grated fresh ginger
½ cup coconut water
4 ice cubes

Put all of the ingredients into a blender and blend until smooth.

MELON & MANGO SOY SMOOTHIE

1 mango, cut into small pieces
2 cups seedless watermelon
½ cup vanilla soy milk
1 tbsp honey
4 ice cubes

Put all of the ingredients into a blender and blend until smooth.

PEAR SOY SMOOTHIE

1 banana
½ cup soy milk
½ cup unsweetened apple juice
¼ cup pear (peeled and chopped)
¼ cup blueberries

Put all of the ingredients into a blender and blend until smooth.

STRAWBERRY BANANA SOY SMOOTHIE

1 cup strawberries
¾ cup vanilla low-fat soy milk
¾ tbsp honey
¼ tsp vanilla extract
1 banana

Put all of the ingredients into a blender and blend until smooth.

Frozen blueberries

Wild Blueberry Smoothie

GREEN
SMOOTHIES

"GREEN SMOOTHIES" AREN'T JUST VEGETABLES—
THEY CAN BE ANY MIXTURE OF FRUITS, VEGETABLES,
OR BOTH, GENERALLY BLENDED WITH FRUIT JUICE OR
WATER TO ACHIEVE THE DESIRED CONSISTENCY, AND
THEY DON'T EVEN NEED TO BE THE COLOR GREEN.
HOWEVER, THE AIM OF THE GREEN-SMOOTHIE, RAW-
FOOD DIET IS TO GET MORE VEGETABLES INTO YOUR
BODY, AS EASILY AS POSSIBLE. SO, IF YOU REALLY DIG
BLUEBERRIES, MAKE ONE OF THE BERRY SMOOTHIES
AND JUST THROW IN A HANDFUL OF SPINACH TO GET
USED TO THE TASTE.

GREEN SMOOTHIES

THE HEALTHIEST ONES

Tired of a juice diet or, perhaps, of cleaning the juicer several times a day? If you want to make a switch, or at least take a break from your routine, you can get all the benefits, including nutrients and healthy weight loss, by throwing the same ingredients in a blender rather than a juicer. Even hard vegetables such as carrots can be cut into small pieces that can be tackled by a blender. Your kids, too, will find smoothies every bit as delicious and scintillating as juices, and easier for them to make. If the smoothie tastes a little too "green" for you, add more fruit until you get used to the taste.

Although juices can be used by diabetics with great success, they must be made with the correct foods—the wrong ingredients (particularly fruits) will lead to a spike in blood sugar level rather than maintenance at a healthy level. In addition, a person who is following a strict juice diet will quickly grow weary of cleaning the juicer several times a day! Green smoothies have been found to be particularly helpful for diabetics across the board: they promote better blood sugar and insulin control, lower blood pressure and cholesterol, facilitate weight loss, contribute to liver and kidney health, and strengthen the immune system.

Kiwi smoothie

Various green smoothies

HEALTHY START

1 cup baby spinach

8 leaves romaine lettuce

2 dates, pitted

1 tbsp sunflower seeds, soaked overnight

1 tbsp sesame seeds, soaked overnight

1 banana

1 cup water

1–2 ounces lemon juice

Wash all produce, then put all of the ingredients into a blender and blend until smooth.

GREEN TOMATOES SMOOTHIE

1 cup fresh parsley

3 stalks celery

3 Roma tomatoes

½ lemon, peeled and seeds removed

½ cup water

2 tbsp dulse flakes

Wash all produce, then put all of the ingredients into a blender and blend until smooth.

SPINACH SMOOTHIE WITH AVOCADO & APPLE

1½ cups apple juice

2 cups stemmed and chopped spinach or kale

1 apple, unpeeled, cored, and chopped

½ avocado, chopped

Combine the apple juice, spinach, apple, and avocado in a blender and puree until smooth, about 1 minute, adding water to reach the desired consistency.

AVOCADO VANILLA SMOOTHIE

1 ripe avocado, chopped

1 cup no-sugar-added pear nectar, plus more as needed

½ tsp pure vanilla extract

1 cup ice cubes

Wash all produce, then puree all of the ingredients in a blender until smooth. If too thick, add more nectar to adjust consistency.

Fresh baby spinach leaves

Spinach Smoothie with Avocado & Apple

APPLE & ALMOND SMOOTHIE

1 apple, sliced
1 cup almond milk
1 handful of spinach
½ tsp cinnamon
pinch of nutmeg
1 cup ice

Wash all produce, then put all of the ingredients into a blender and blend until smooth. Garnish with a pinch of cinnamon and enjoy.

APPLE-LEMONADE SMOOTHIE

1 cup water (or ½ cup water and ½ cup ice)
1 lemon, peeled and seeded
1 apple, cored, peeled and sliced
1 banana
1–2 cups baby spinach
a little honey, stevia, or maple syrup to sweeten (optional)
½ inch ginger (optional)

Wash all produce, then put all of the ingredients into a blender and blend until smooth.

PINEAPPLE YOGURT SPINACH

¼ cup plain non-fat Greek yogurt or a non-dairy alternative
1 tbsp honey
2 cups lightly packed baby spinach
½ large apple, chunked
handful of (about 20) raw almonds
1 cup frozen pineapple
3–4 ice cubes
1 cup unsweetened almond milk

Wash all produce, then put all of the ingredients into a blender and blend until smooth.

APPLE-GRAPE SMOOTHIE

2 medium-size apples (unpeeled and sliced)
6–10 seedless grapes
1 tbsp of Greek yogurt
½ cup of fresh milk (high calcium, low fat)
4–6 ice cubes

Wash the apples and grapes and drop them into a blender, pour in the milk and the yogurt, add the ice cubes, and then blend until smooth.

PINEAPPLE-MANGO

1 cup frozen pineapple
1 cup frozen mango pieces
1 cup vanilla yogurt
⅓ cup milk (or more if needed)
2 tsp sugar
2 ice cubes (optional)

Place all of the ingredients in a blender and blend until smooth. Add more milk if too thick or ice if too thin.

PINEAPPLE-COCONUT

1 cup fresh pineapple, chopped
¼ cup coconut milk
¼ cup vanilla (or coconut!) flavored yogurt
1 tbsp sweetened flaked coconut
3–4 ice cubes (optional)

Blend all ingredients until smooth. Serve with additional flaked coconut on top.

Apple & Almond Smoothie

BANANA PINEAPPLE SPINACH SMOOTHIE

2 cups pineapple, cut into chunks

1 cup (8 oz) vanilla almond milk or coconut milk

2 ripe bananas, peeled and sliced

1–2 cups baby spinach

1 cup crushed ice

2 tbsp shredded toasted coconut (optional)

Blend all ingredients. Garnish with additional pineapple and toasted coconut, if desired.

BLUE-GREEN SMOOTHIE

1 bunch dandelion greens

1 bunch fresh parsley

1 cup fresh blueberries

1 pear

3 cups water

Wash all the produce, then put all of the ingredients into a blender and blend until smooth.

KALE, ORANGE & BANANA

1 orange, peeled

½ cup water

1 leaf kale, torn into several pieces

2 ripe bananas, peeled

Put all of the ingredients into a blender and blend until smooth.

BANANA BLUEBERRY SMOOTHIE

1 large ripe banana, sliced

½ cup blueberries, frozen or fresh

2 cups spinach

½ cup low-fat vanilla yogurt

1½ cups ice cubes

In a blender, combine banana, blueberries, spinach, and yogurt until smooth. Add ice cubes and blend until crushed and well combined. Pour into glasses and serve immediately.

PEACHES & CREAM GREEN SMOOTHIE

1 cup almond milk

1 banana

2 cups spinach

1¼ cup frozen peach slices

Wash all the produce, then put all of the ingredients into a blender and blend until smooth.

CARROT-APRICOT SMOOTHIE

2 apricots

1 apple

2 cups fresh baby spinach (or other leafy green)

2 whole carrots

½ cup water

Wash all the produce, then put all of the ingredients into a blender and blend until smooth.

Banana Blueberry Smoothie

ORANGE & BLACKCURRANT SMOOTHIE

1 pint blackcurrants
1 ripe mango
1 head butter lettuce
2 cups orange juice

Wash all the produce, then put all of the ingredients into a blender and blend until smooth.

ORANGE-BANANA SMOOTHIE

1 large orange, peeled and segmented
½ banana, cut into chunks
6 large strawberries
2 cups spinach
⅓ cup plain Greek yogurt

Wash all the produce, then put all of the ingredients into a blender and blend until smooth.

CITRUS ENERGY-BLAST SMOOTHIE

1 orange, peeled and chopped, seeds removed
1 lemon, peeled and chopped, seeds removed
6 spinach leaves
2 carrots, peeled and chopped (or grated)
1½ cup almond milk
1 peach, peeled and chopped

Wash all the produce, then put all of the ingredients into a blender and blend until smooth.

ORANGE SMOOTHIE

2 cups arugula
½ orange bell pepper
2 oranges, peeled and seeded
1 banana to make it sweeter, if desired

Wash all the produce, then put all of the ingredients into a blender and blend until smooth.

ORANGE & GREEN SMOOTHIE

2 cups spinach, packed
1 mango
2 oranges, peeled and seeded
1 sprig fresh rosemary, leaves only

Wash all the produce, then put all of the ingredients into a blender and blend until smooth.

Fresh peaches

Citrus Energy-blast Smoothie

GREEN MAGIC

6 romaine leaves, chopped

4 kale leaves, chopped

½ cup fresh parsley sprigs

½ cup chopped pineapple

½ cup chopped mango

1 inch fresh ginger, peeled and chopped

Wash all the produce, then put all of the ingredients into a blender and blend until smooth.

PLUM-BANANA SMOOTHIE

2 plums, deseeded

1 banana, peeled

2 cups fresh baby spinach (or other leafy green)

½ vine tomato

½–1 cup water, depending on desired consistency

Wash all the produce, then put all of the ingredients into a blender and blend until smooth.

PLUM-MANGO-SPINACH SMOOTHIE

½ mango

1 carrot

2 cups fresh baby spinach

2 plums

1 cup water

Add ice as needed

Wash all the produce, then put all of the ingredients into a blender and blend until smooth.

SPINACH & STRAWBERRY SMOOTHIE

1 cup water

1 cup spinach

3 cups strawberries

1 cup oats

¼ cup cashew nuts

7 leaves mint

Wash all produce, then blend the ingredients in the order listed, and only a few at a time. If you don't have a powerful blender and want the smoothie very smooth, soak the oats for an hour before blending. If it gets too thick, add more water as necessary.

SPICY SMOOTHIE

2 cups spinach

12 cloves garlic

juice of 1 lemon

½ cucumber (add more if the smoothie is two hot)

¼ tsp cayenne pepper

½ tsp minced jalapeño pepper

1 cup water

Wash all the produce, then put all of the ingredients into a blender and blend until smooth.

PLUM-WATERMELON SMOOTHIE

2 plums, deseeded

2 cups watermelon

1 banana

2 cups fresh baby spinach (or other leafy green)

2 celery stalks, chopped

½ cup water if needed

Wash all the produce, then put all of the ingredients into a blender and blend until smooth.

Plum-Watermelon Smoothie

GRAPEFRUIT WITH APPLE & KIWI SMOOTHIE

1 grapefruit

1 kiwi

1 apple

1 medium banana

2 cups low-fat milk

2 tbsp low fat vanilla yogurt

1 tsp peanut butter

1 tsp flax seed

3 ice cubes

Wash all the produce, then put all of the ingredients into a blender and blend until smooth.

TANGERINE-PAPAYA SMOOTHIE

2 tangerines, peeled and deseeded

2 cups papaya, cubed

2 cups fresh baby spinach (or other leafy green)

8 ounces of water or tangerine juice

Wash all the produce, then put all of the ingredients into a blender and blend until smooth.

BANANA-GRAPEFRUIT-KALE SMOOTHIE

4–5 kale leaves, chopped

2 large ripe bananas, fresh or frozen

1 grapefruit, peeled and cut

1 cup water

Wash all the produce, then put all of the ingredients into a blender and blend until smooth.

TANGERINE-COCONUT SMOOTHIE

2 tangerines, peeled and deseeded

1 young green or Thai coconut

1 banana (or 2 cups papaya, cubed)

2 cups fresh baby spinach (or other leafy green)

2 celery stalks (optional)

4–6 ounces of coconut water

Wash all the produce, then put all of the ingredients into a blender and blend until smooth.

CITRUS-MANGO SMOOTHIE

1½ mangoes

½ cup pineapple chunks

⅓ cup strawberries

2 large handfuls of organic baby spinach

1 banana

1 orange

1 tbsp agave nectar

⅓ cup water

1 cup ice

Wash all the produce, then put all of the ingredients into a blender and blend until smooth.

KALE-ORANGE SMOOTHIE

1 cup kale

1 cup orange juice

2 tbsp mint leaves

2 tbsp cilantro

2 tbsp parsley

1 cup ice

Wash all the produce, then put all of the ingredients into a blender and blend until smooth.

Grapefruit with Apple & Kiwi Smoothie

KALE, PINEAPPLE, ALMOND-MILK SMOOTHIE

1 banana, sliced into chunks, frozen is ideal

1 heaping cup fresh pineapple chunks

1 giant handful of coarsely chopped kale leaves, center rib removed

1 cup cold almond milk

1 tbsp honey (optional, for added sweetness)

Wash all the produce, then put all of the ingredients into a blender and blend until smooth.

SWEET & SOUR SMOOTHIE

1 cup collard greens, stems removed

½ cup alfalfa sprouts

½ pineapple

1 banana

3 Medjool dates, pitted

3 tbsp lemon juice

1 cup water

Wash all the produce, then put all of the ingredients into a blender and blend until smooth.

SPINACH-KALE-PEAR SMOOTHIE

1 heaping cup spinach leaves

1 heaping cup chopped kale leaves

½ pear

1 frozen banana

1½ cups cold almond milk (or soy milk or orange juice)

1 tbsp honey

Wash all produce, then remove kale leaves from their rough center stalk and coarsely chop. In a blender, combine kale, spinach, and almond milk. Blend until no big kale bits remain. Stop blender and add banana, honey, and pear. Blend until smooth.

STAR FRUIT & PINEAPPLE SMOOTHIE

1 cup pineapple chunks

1 cup star fruit chunks

1 cup pineapple guava chunks

1 banana

½ bunch chard

2 cups water

Wash all the produce, then put all of the ingredients into a blender and blend until smooth.

BLUEBERRY, YOGURT & KALE SMOOTHIE

2 cups frozen blueberries

1 tbsp Greek yogurt

2–3 cups nonfat milk

1 banana

1 cup kale

honey (drizzled to taste)

flaxseed (optional)

Wash all the produce, then put all of the ingredients into a blender and blend until smooth.

WHITE PEACH, ORANGE & ROMAINE SMOOTHIE

2 oranges, peeled and chopped

1 white peach, pitted and chopped

4–6 large romaine lettuce leaves

1 cup ice

Wash all produce, then add oranges to blender, followed by peach, romaine, and ice. Blend on high until smooth.

Star Fruit & Pineapple Smoothie

DANDELAPPLE SMOOTHIE

3 cups dandelion greens, freshly picked
2 cups apple juice
1 cup water
1 fresh mango
1 ripe peach

Wash all the produce, then put all of the ingredients into a blender and blend until smooth.

ROMAINE-WATERMELON

4 cups fresh watermelon chunks, rind removed
1 banana
5 leaves romaine lettuce
juice of ½ lemon

Wash all the produce, then put all of the ingredients into a blender and blend until smooth.

STAR FRUIT-BANANA

1 large star fruit, deseeded
1 banana, peeled
½ tsp pure vanilla extract
2 cups fresh baby spinach or other leafy green
8 ounces of filtered water or coconut water

Wash all the produce, then put all of the ingredients into a blender and blend until smooth.

STRAWBERRY-MANGO SMOOTHIE

2½ cups strawberries
1 cup pineapple
1 large ripe mango, peeled
½–1 head romaine lettuce
8 ounces filtered water

Wash all the produce, then start by adding the liquid to your blender, followed by the soft fruit. Add the greens to your blender last. Blend on high for 30 seconds or until the smoothie is creamy.

SWEET ROMAINE SMOOTHIE

1 cup ice
1 cup non-dairy milk
1 cup strawberries
1 banana or 1 cup of mango chunks or 1 small mango
1 cup pineapple
1 apple
1 cup chopped romaine lettuce
2 tbsp pumpkin seeds
½ cup dried apricots
1 cup of oats

Wash all produce, then blend the ingredients in the order listed. Ground the oats into flour to make it smoother. Add more water if required to thin it out.

Dandelapple Smoothie

Freshly cut dandelion leaves

PROTEIN

SMOOTHIES

USE ANY OF THESE RECIPES TO START YOUR DAY, FUEL UP BEFORE A WORKOUT, OR REPLENISH YOUR MUSCLES AFTER YOU'VE FINISHED TRAINING. IN ANY OF THE FOLLOWING SHAKES, FEEL FREE TO ADD 1 TABLESPOON OF GROUND FLAXSEED AND GO WITH EXTRA ICE OR NO ICE.

PROTEIN SMOOTHIES

Scoops of whey protein isolate and egg white powder sound like odd ingredients in a book of raw foods, specifically juices and smoothies designed to make up for an inability to consume the recommended number of servings a day. However, these are standard—and essential—ingredients in many protein smoothies. Both are dried forms of protein-rich material, milk and egg whites respectively, and jump-start your morning. Protein smoothies are particularly conceived to give a burst of energy to get going (or, indeed, before a body-building workout or any other physical exercise), and have been credited in increases in lean muscle.

APPETIZER SMOOTHIES

Some smoothies and juices are nearly identical in ingredients and texture, although not, of course, in texture, gazpacho among them. Others make fun after-school snacks for your kids and their friends, such as the Funky Monkey Smoothie. But chilled creations of cucumber or zucchini blended with a plethora of herbs are special treats that you may want to save for company or a special occasion; likewise, smoothies spiked with alcohol are not for the younger set.

BURN

1½ cups water or unsweetened almond milk

2 scoops egg white powder or whey protein isolate

8 strawberries

1 tbsp raw almond butter or ground flaxseed

6 ice cubes

Mix in a blender for 30 seconds.

DADDY SHAKE

1½ cups fresh orange juice

2 scoops egg white powder or whey protein isolate

1 banana

2 tbsp almond butter or natural peanut butter

6 ice cubes

Shake, stir, or blend.

RISE & SHINE SMOOTHIE

1½–2 cups fresh squeezed orange juice

2 scoops egg white powder or vanilla whey protein powder

1 banana

¼ cup Greek yogurt

2 tsp organic vanilla extract

1 tbsp ground flaxseed (optional)

1 tbsp lecithin (optional)

Blend together for 30 seconds.

PRE-WORKOUT SHAKE

1–1½ cups water

1 banana

4 ice cubes

Mix in a blender for 30 seconds.

TROPICAL SURPRISE SHAKE

1½ cups water or orange juice

1 scoop whey protein isolate

¼ cup each of as many fruits as you can find in the fridge

1 banana

6 ice cubes

Mix in a blender for 30 seconds.

BLUEBERRY BOOST

1 cup unsweetened vanilla almond milk

1 frozen banana

½ cup blueberries

1 scoop unflavored or vanilla protein powder

Mix in a blender for 30 seconds.

Pre-workout Shake

TROPICAL BOOST

1 cup unsweetened vanilla almond milk

1 cup frozen pineapple

1 tsp shredded coconut or coconut milk

½ cup frozen blueberries

1 scoop unflavored or vanilla protein powder

Mix in a blender for 30 seconds.

PEANUT BUTTER BANANA SMOOTHIE

1 cup frozen banana, sliced

1 oz natural peanut butter

½ cup 1% milk

1 tbsp honey

Combine all ingredients in a blender. Blend until smooth. Refrigerate or serve immediately.

WATERMELON MINT

1 cup watermelon, cubed

½ cup liquid egg whites

mint sprigs

crushed ice

Wash all produce, then add all ingredients to a blender. Blend, pour, and enjoy.

CHOCOLATE CHIP CREAMY SMOOTHIE

1 cup unsweetened chocolate almond milk

1 tbsp natural almond or peanut butter

1 frozen banana (peel before freezing)

1 tbsp cacao nibs

1 cup raw spinach

1 scoop chocolate protein powder

dash of red pepper flakes (optional)

Wash all produce, then mix in a blender for 30 seconds.

PIÑA COLADA PROTEIN SMOOTHIE

½ cup pineapple, chopped

½ frozen banana

1 scoop vanilla protein

½ cup unsweetened coconut milk

½ cup water

crushed ice

Add all ingredients to a blender. Blend, pour, and enjoy.

STRAWBERRY PAPAYA SMOOTHIE

½ cup strawberries

1 cup papaya, sliced

1 cup non-fat plain Greek yogurt

½ cup water

crushed ice

Wash all produce, then add all ingredients to a blender. Blend, pour, and enjoy.

Watermelon Mint

CRANBERRY-COCO BLAST

1 tbsp dried, unsweetened cranberries
½ cup frozen cherries
½ tbsp chia seeds
½ tbsp flaxseeds
⅓ cup non-fat plain Greek yogurt
½ cup unsweetened coconut milk
crushed ice

Add all ingredients to a blender. Blend, pour, and enjoy.

CRANBERRY-ORANGE POWER SMOOTHIE

1 cup cranberry juice
1 large banana
1 medium orange, peeled and segmented
½ cup strawberries, hulled
¼ cup raspberry sherbet
1 cup ice cubes
¼ cup whey protein powder

Place all ingredients in a blender. Blend on high speed until smooth, about one minute. Adjust the consistency by adding more sherbet if it's too thin, or more cranberry juice if it's too thick. Pour into two glasses and use a straw!

STRAWBERRY BANANA PROTEIN SMOOTHIE

1 banana
1¼ cups sliced fresh strawberries
10 whole almonds
2 tbsp water
1 cup ice cubes
3 tbsp chocolate flavored protein powder

Place the banana, strawberries, almonds, and water into a blender. Blend to mix, then add the ice cubes and puree until smooth. Add the protein powder, and continue mixing until evenly incorporated, about 30 seconds.

COCO-MANGO COOL DOWN

1 cup chopped mango
½ cup unsweetened coconut milk
1 scoop vanilla protein powder

Add all ingredients to a blender. Blend, pour, and enjoy.

PEANUT BOOST

1 scoop vanilla protein powder
6 oz unsweetened almond milk (or milk of choice)
3–4 ice cubes
1 tbsp natural chunky peanut butter
1 tbsp sugar-free instant butterscotch pudding mix

Add all ingredients to a blender. Blend, pour, and enjoy.

COOLATTA SHAKE

1 scoop chocolate or vanilla whey protein powder
6 oz unsweetened almond milk (or milk of choice)
4 ice cubes
1 tbsp Nutella
1–2 tsp instant coffee

Add all ingredients to a blender. Blend, pour, and enjoy.

Coco-Mango Cool Down

POWER PROTEIN SUPER SMOOTHIE

2 cups mixed berries, fresh or frozen
1 cup silken tofu
¼ cup pomegranate juice
2 to 3 tbsp honey
2 tbsp ground flaxseed
1 tsp finely grated peeled ginger

In a blender, combine berries, tofu, pomegranate juice, 2 tablespoons honey, flaxseed, and ginger. Blend until smooth, 15 to 20 seconds. Adjust the sweetness if necessary.

STAY-YOUTHFUL SMOOTHIE

½ cup frozen organic blueberries
½ cup frozen organic strawberries
½ cup chilled green tea, unsweetened
¾ cup plain low-fat organic yogurt
2 tbsp ground flaxseed
turbinado sugar or other natural sweetener to taste

Combine all ingredients in a blender and blend on medium speed until smooth, about 20 seconds. Garnish with fresh berries and serve. Note: For a nondairy alternative, you can substitute cultured soy for the yogurt.

STRAWBERRY-BANANA TOFU SHAKE

1 package (10 ounces) frozen, unsweetened strawberries, thawed
1 cup plain soymilk
1 small ripe banana, peeled and sliced
¼ cup honey
1 package (12 ounces) silken soft tofu, drained
2 tbsp fresh lemon juice
pinch of salt

In a blender, puree berries until smooth. Remove, and rinse blender. Combine the remaining ingredients in the blender. Puree until smooth and thoroughly mixed, scraping down sides with rubber spatula as necessary. Divide among glasses and spoon strawberry puree on one side of each glass.

CHERRY-TEA SMOOTHIE

¾ cup water
2 Rooibos tea bags
6 ounces silken tofu
2 cups frozen sweet cherries
2 cups grapes
½ cup frozen blueberries

Bring water to a simmer and steep tea bags for two minutes. Allow to cool. Add tea to tofu and fruit, and puree.

FRUIT & YOGURT SMOOTHIE

1½ cups plain nonfat or low-fat yogurt
½ medium chopped peeled pear
1 small sliced banana
2 tbsp protein powder
¾ cup crushed ice

Add all ingredients to a blender. Blend, pour, and enjoy.

CRANBERRY PROTEIN SMOOTHIE

1¼ cups unsweetened cranberry juice
2 scoops Lisa Lynn's Complete French Vanilla Protein Powder
5 ice cubes

Place all ingredients in the jar of a blender. Blend until well combined; serve immediately.

Cherry-Tea Smoothie

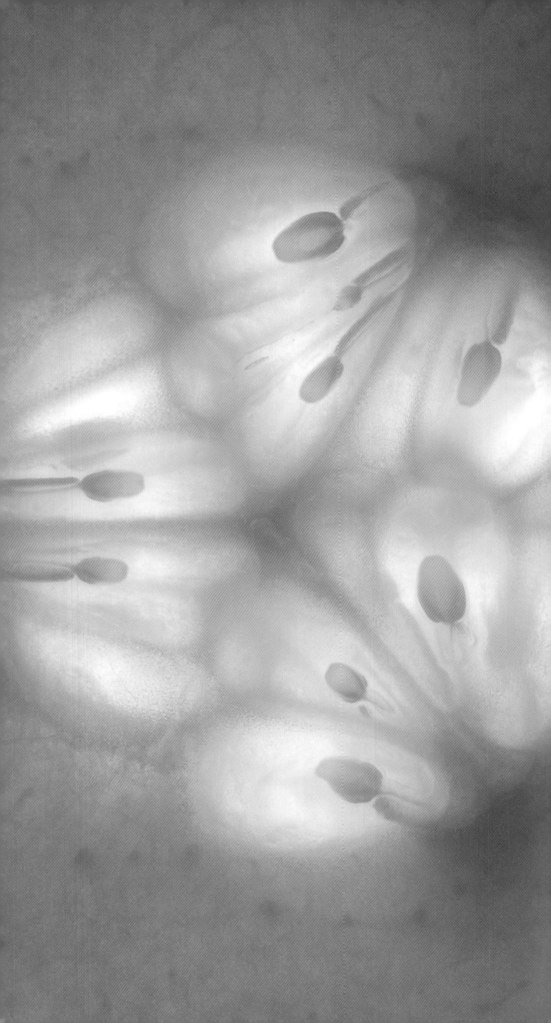

APPETIZER
SMOOTHIES

A SMOOTHIE CAN BE A SOPHISTICATED STARTER

AT YOUR NEXT DINNER PARTY. VICHYSSOISE,

OR A VARIETY OF FRUIT- OR VEGETABLE-BASED

CONCOCTIONS CAN BE SERVED IN A BOWL WITH

A SPOON, WHILE PINEAPPLE AND LEMON JUICE

COMBINED WITH SPARKLING WINE MAKE A

DELICIOUS COCKTAIL. TO ACHIEVE THEIR SUBTLETY,

THESE RECIPES HAVE MORE INGREDIENTS THAN

MOST OF THE OTHER SMOOTHIES IN THIS BOOK.

PUMPKIN SMOOTHIE

1 cup non-dairy milk, such as unsweetened almond milk
½ cup canned pumpkin
½ banana
1 tbsp raisins or ½ tsp maple syrup
½ tsp pure vanilla extract
¼ tsp ground cinnamon
⅛ tsp ground ginger
pinch of ground nutmeg
pinch of ground cloves
pinch of allspice

Blend until smooth and top with coconut whipped topping and cinnamon.

LA VIDA LOCA

½ cup strawberries
1 tsp stevia
1 tbsp water
1 cup coconut milk
½ cup pineapple
2 scoops nutritional shake mix
1 tsp rum extract

Puree strawberries with stevia and water. Add a little more water if necessary. Pour into a glass and swirl around to cover half the glass.
   Place coconut milk, pineapple, protein powder, and rum extract with a few ice cubes. Puree and pour into the glass. Top with a strawberry for presentation.

CASHEW DELIGHT

1 cup boiling water
1 cup raw cashews
1 cup ice
1 vanilla bean, seeds scraped (reserve the bean itself for another use), or 1 tsp pure vanilla extract
1 tbsp agave nectar

Pour boiling water over cashews and let stand until softened, about 15 minutes.
   Puree in a blender on high speed for 3 minutes until smooth.
   Add ice and vanilla extract or seeds. Blend until smooth. Add agave nectar to taste.

CHOCOLATE PEANUT BUTTER SMOOTHIE

1 banana
2 tbsp unsweetened cocoa powder
1 tbsp vanilla-flavored protein powder
¼ cup chunky or creamy peanut butter
1½ cups vanilla-flavored milk alternative such as almond or soy
handful of ice cubes

Put all of the ingredients into a blender and blend until smooth.

PEAR, OAT, CINNAMON & GINGER SMOOTHIE

2 large ripe pears, chopped
¾ cup milk or non-dairy milk substitute
6 oz yogurt (I used 0% fat Greek yogurt)
¼ cup rolled oats
5–7 ice cubes
½ inch ginger
½ tsp cinnamon
pinch of kosher salt

Put all of the ingredients into a blender and blend until smooth.

CHAMOMILE-BANANA SMOOTHIE

1 cup strong chamomile tea, room temperature
1 ripe banana
1 cup low-fat plain yogurt
2 tbsp maple syrup

Freeze chamomile tea in an ice cube tray. Combine with remaining ingredients in a blender, and blend until smooth.

Pumpkin Smoothie

Freshly picked red cabbage

Chia seeds

GODZILLA SMOOTHIE

16 oz unsweetened coconut or almond milk

4 tbsp almond butter or other nut butter

2 tsp raw honey

3 tbsp cocoa powder

2 bananas

2 tsp vanilla

Place all the ingredients in a blender and blend. If you are using unfrozen bananas, then add 8 ice cubes. Makes enough for 2 so share it with your family or friends.

RICH CHOCOLATE SMOOTHIE

1 banana, frozen

¾ cup milk

1 tbsp sugar

1 tsp chia seeds

¼ tsp cocoa

1 tbsp Greek yogurt

1–2 tbsp peanut butter

1–2 tsp chocolate syrup

6 ice cubes

Place all the ingredients in a blender and blend.

PURPLE DELIGHT

2 cups red cabbage

1 cup blueberries

2 bananas

2 tbsp chia seeds

½ cup water

Soak chia seeds in water for 10 minutes before blending. Place all ingredients into a blender in the following order: cabbage, blueberries, banana, chia seeds, water. Blend to a smooth consistency. Pour into glass and serve!

Purple Delight

CHOCOLATE-CHIP SMOOTHIE

¼ cup raw pecans

¼ cups Medjool dates, pitted (about 3–4 large fruits)

1 large ripe pear, chopped

2 tbsp lucuma powder

1 tsp maca powder

1½ cups unsweetened almond milk

2 tbsp cacao nibs

2 cups coconut ice cubes (freeze coconut water in ice-cube trays)

sugar, to taste (optional)

Blend together all the ingredients except the cacao nibs and coconut ice until creamy and smooth. Add the nibs and ice and blend until frosty; the nibs will serve as the "chocolate chips" and add a crunchy kick.

FUNNY MONKEY SMOOTHIE

1 large banana, frozen

1 tbsp peanut butter

1 tbsp chocolate syrup or 1 tbsp powdered chocolate milk mix

¼ cup skim milk

¼ cup ice cubes

Put all of the ingredients into a blender and blend until smooth.

Chocolate-Chip Smoothie

Medjool dates

Ripe pears

Maca powder

Cacao nibs

SPARKLING WINE & PINEAPPLE

2 cups sparkling wine

3 cups pineapple, freshly grated

2 tbsp lemon juice

toasted coconut

Combine sparkling wine, pineapple flesh, and lemon juice in a bowl; stir gently, and serve immediately. Garnish: toasted coconut.

MELON & MINT DELIGHT

2 cups yogurt

¼ cup milk

1 cup mint leaves, chopped

1 medium-sized, ripe cantaloupe or honeydew melon

2 tbsp lime juice

1 tsp chili powder

pistachios

In a bowl, whisk together yogurt, milk, and mint leaves until mint is fragrant; strain and discard solids. In another bowl, combine the grated flesh of the melon, lime juice, and chili powder; refrigerate bowls for 2 hours, stirring once. To serve, spoon yogurt onto melon and stir. Garnish: chopped pistachios.

STRAWBERRY-ORANGE

2 cups yogurt

¼ cup orange juice

1 cup mint leaves, chopped

1 tbsp sugar

2 cups strawberries, sliced

2 tbsp lime juice

1 tsp chili powder

whipped cream

In a bowl, whisk together yogurt, orange juice, chopped mint leaves, and sugar until mint is fragrant; strain and discard solids. In another bowl, combine strawberries, lime juice, sugar, and chili powder; refrigerate bowls for 2 hours, stirring once. To serve, spoon yogurt onto strawberries and stir. Garnish: whipped cream and mint.

Honeydew melon

Melon & Mint Delight

CHILLY CUCUMBER

2 cups Greek yogurt

1 cup vegetable broth

2 English cucumbers, peeled, diced, and divided

4 green onions, sliced, divided

2 tbsp fresh dill, chopped

2 tbsp fresh parsley, chopped

4 tsp fresh lemon juice (a little over 1/3 lemon)

2 tsp salt

In a large bowl, combine Greek yogurt and vegetable broth; set aside. In a food processor, puree 1 English cucumber, 2 green onions, dill, and parsley. Add the cucumber mixture, lemon juice, and salt to the yogurt mixture; whisk to combine. Stir in 1 more English cucumber and 2 more green onions; refrigerate for 1 hour. Garnish each serving with chopped dill and croutons.

CHILLY ZUCCHINI

3 tbsp extra-virgin olive oil

1 small onion

2 garlic cloves

1 tsp thyme leaves

1 bay leaf

8 small zucchini (3 pounds), plus long zucchini shavings for garnish

3 cups water

2 tbsp finely shredded basil

2 cups of baby arugala, chopped

2 cups ice

pinch of salt

freshly ground pepper

Heat the 2 tablespoons of olive oil in a large saucepan. Add the garlic and onion and cook over moderate heat until the onion is translucent. Stir in the bay leaf and thyme and cook until fragrant—about 1 minute. Add the sliced zucchini, season with salt and cook, stirring occasionally, until tender—about 10 minutes. Add the water and bring to a boil. Remove the saucepan from the heat. Discard the bay leaf and stir in the shredded basil.

Working in batches, puree in a blender until smooth. Transfer the zucchini puree to a large bowl and stir in the ice. Refrigerate the puree for at least 3 hours, until thoroughly chilled.

Season with salt and pepper. Ladle into shallow bowls and top with a small handful of baby arugula and zucchini shavings. Drizzle with olive oil and serve.

Green onions

Chilly Cucumber

VICHYSSOISE SMOOTHIE

2 tbsp butter
3 potatoes, peeled and cubed
3 leeks, trimmed and chopped
4 cups stock
½ cup cream
chives

Wash all produce, then melt butter in a large pot. Add potatoes and leeks. Cook for about 3 minutes, stirring, until softened. Add stock. Boil, cover, lower the heat, and simmer until vegetables are tender, about 20 minutes. Puree, then let cool. Stir in cream before serving. Garnish: chopped chives.

VICHYSSOISE AVOCADO

2 tbsp butter
1 or 2 avocados, coarsely chopped
3 potatoes, peeled and cubed
3 leeks, trimmed and chopped
4 cups stock
cilantro

Wash all produce, then melt butter in a large pot. Add potatoes and leeks, and cook for about 3 minutes, stirring. Add stock; boil, cover, and simmer for 20 minutes until vegetables are tender. Puree, then let cool; stir in avocados before serving. Garnish: chopped cilantro.

VICHYSSOISE GARDEN-GREENS

2 tbsp butter
3 potatoes, peeled and cubed
2 cups fresh spinach or other greens, or 1–2 zucchini, cubed
4 cups stock
½ cup cream
olive oil

Wash all produce, then melt butter in a large pot. Add potatoes, fresh spinach, greens or zucchini. Cook for about 3 minutes, stirring, until softened. Add 4 cups stock. Boil, cover, lower the heat and simmer until vegetables are tender, about 20 minutes. Puree, then let cool. Stir in ½ cup or more cream before serving. Garnish: Olive oil.

Vichyssoise Smoothie

Potatoes and leeks

PUREED FENNEL

1½ lbs fennel, trimmed and chopped
1 onion, peeled and chopped
2 tbsp butter
5 cups stock or water
chervil

Wash all produce. Sauté fennel and onion in butter to soften, about 5 minutes. Add stock or water; boil, cover, lower the heat and simmer until fennel is tender, about 15 minutes. Cool slightly, puree, strain and refrigerate. Garnish: chopped chervil.

PUREED CARROT

1½ lbs carrots, trimmed and chopped
1 onion, peeled and chopped
2 tbsp butter
5 cups stock or water
parsley

Wash all produce. Sauté carrots and onion in butter to soften, about 5 minutes. Add stock or water; boil, cover, lower the heat and simmer until carrots are tender, about 15 minutes. Cool slightly, purée and refrigerate. Garnish: chopped parsley.

PUREED ASPARAGUS

5 cups stock or water
1½ lbs asparagus, chopped
1 large potato, peeled and cubed
lemon juice
olive oil

Wash all produce. Add stock or water to asparagus (peeled if it's thick) and potato; boil, cover, lower the heat and simmer until the asparagus is tender, about 15 minutes. Cool slightly, puree and refrigerate. Garnish: lemon juice and olive oil.

Fresh parsley

Pureed Carrot

TOMATO GAZPACHO

2 lbs tomatoes, chopped

1 cucumber, peeled and diced

¼ cup olive oil

2 slices day-old bread

1 tbsp garlic, minced

Combine tomatoes with cucumber, olive oil, day-old bread, and garlic in a food processor or blender; process until chunky-smooth. Garnish: olive oil.

RADISH GAZPACHO

1 lb tomatoes, chopped

1 lb radishes with leaves, chopped

1 cucumber, peeled and diced

¼ cup olive oil

1 slice day-old bread

a few scallions, chopped

2 tbsp lime juice

¼ tsp Worcestershire sauce

Combine tomatoes and radishes (with leaves if they're nice) with cucumber, olive oil, day-old bread, scallions, lime juice, Worcestershire sauce, and water as needed in a food processor or blender; process until chunky-smooth. Garnish: fresh lime juice.

WATERMELON GAZPACHO

½ lb tomatoes, chopped

1½ lbs watermelon, seeded and cubed

1 cucumber, peeled and diced

1 handful of mint leaves

¼ cup olive oil

2 tbsp lemon juice

feta

Combine tomatoes with watermelon, cucumber, mint leaves, and olive oil in a food processor or blender; process until chunky-smooth. Add lemon juice. Garnish: crumbled feta and chopped mint.

Watermelon Gazpacho

Feta

Tomato Gazpacho

DESSERT

SMOOTHIES

YES, YOU CAN HAVE YOUR SMOOTHIE AND EAT IT
TOO. THE BLENDER THAT HAS PRODUCED NUTRITIOUS
SMOOTHIES ALL DAY LONG HAS BEEN REPURPOSED TO
PROVIDE A SOURCE OF ELEGANT—NOT TO MENTION
THOROUGHLY DECADENT—CONCOCTIONS FOR DESSERT.
WHETHER YOU CRAVE CHOCOLATE OR WISH TO SERVE
A SOPHISTICATED TIRAMISU TO YOUR GUESTS, THE
FOLLOWING RECIPES WILL HELP YOU EXPLORE THE
MORE HEDONISTIC USES OF YOUR BLENDER.

NEAPOLITAN NIGHTS SMOOTHIE

1 cup whole milk
1 scoop chocolate ice cream
½ cup strawberries
toasted coconut; to decorate

Place the milk, chocolate ice cream, and strawberries into your blender and process until smooth. Pour into glass and top with strawberry and toasted coconut.

LIME, CHILI & CHOCOLATE SMOOTHIE

2 cups dairy-free milk
1 cup water
1 cup berries, fresh or frozen, a mixture or just one type
2 bananas, frozen
1 cup oats
2 cups spinach or other mild green
¼ cup almonds (whole or ground)
3 tbsp cocoa or carob powder
½ cup raisins, dates, or date paste
½ tsp cayenne pepper, chili powder, or fresh chili to taste
juice of 4 limes

Just put all the ingredients in the blender together and blend well until smooth.

CHOCOLATE TRUFFLE SMOOTHIE

1 cup strong chocolate truffle coffee, chilled
½ cup whole milk
1 scoop vanilla ice cream
a few ice cubes
½–2 tsp coffee syrup or whipped cream, to decorate
grated chocolate; to decorate

Place the coffee, milk, and ice cream in your blender and process until smooth. Pour into glass with a little ice and sweeten to taste with the coffee syrup. Top with a swirl of the whipped cream and decorate with the grated chocolate.

NUTTY CHOCOLATE SMOOTHIE

1 cup whole milk
1 scoop chocolate ice cream
2 tbsp mixed chopped nuts
2 tbsp mini marshmallows
1 tbsp mini marshmallows (optional, to decorate)

Combine the milk, chocolate ice cream, 2 tbsp mini marshmallows, and chopped nuts into your smoothie blender and process until smooth.
    Pour into glass and optionally top with mini marshmallows.

UTTERLY DELICIOUS CHOCOLATE SMOOTHIE

1 cup whole milk
1 scoop chocolate ice cream
sliced strawberries for decoration

Pour the milk and add the ice cream into the blender and process until smooth. Garnish with sliced strawberries.

CHOCOLATE RASPBERRY SMOOTHIE

1 cup fresh raspberries
1 banana
2 tbsp cocoa
1 cup vanilla ice cream
1 cup milk

Cut up the banana first, then add the rest of the ingredients. If you prefer your smoothie cold, add some ice to the blender. Blend until smooth. The banana gives the smoothie a thicker consistency, but if you don't like that flavor, leave it out.

Chocolate Truffle Smoothie

PEANUT BUTTER SMOOTHIE

2 cups milk or chocolate milk
¼ cup peanut butter
¼ cup chocolate syrup
3 scoops chocolate frozen yogurt
1 tbsp miniature peanut butter cups or chocolate chips.

In a blender, combine milk, peanut butter, and chocolate syrup and blend again until smooth. Add the chocolate frozen yogurt and blend, then pour into chilled glasses. Sprinkle with peanut butter cups or chocolate chips.

PEANUT SPLIT SMOOTHIE

1 banana
2 tbsp peanut butter
1–2 tbsp chocolate syrup
1 tbsp wheat germ
6 oz milk

Put the banana in the blender first, then add the rest of the ingredients. If you prefer your smoothie cold, add some ice to the blender. Blend until smooth. If you're feeling adventuresome, you can substitute any other nut butter for the peanut butter.

CARAMEL SMOOTHIE

½ cup whole milk
1 scoop rich chocolate ice cream
2 scoops vanilla ice cream
2 tbsp semisweet chocolate chips
1 tbsp butterscotch sauce, plus extra for decoration
peanuts or almonds to decorate

Place the milk, chocolate ice cream, 1 scoop of vanilla ice cream, and butterscotch sauce into your blender and process until smooth. Pour into a glass, then stir in the chocolate chips.

Top with the remaining vanilla ice cream and drizzle over it with plenty of butterscotch sauce. Sprinkle with the chopped nuts.

CHOCOMONSTER SMOOTHIE

1–2 frozen bananas
¼ cup raw cacao powder
⅓ cup raw almond butter
2 pitted dates
½–1 cup raw almond milk

Freezing the bananas before use will give the creamy texture. Add all ingredients to the blender, then blend until smooth; it will be thick, like a chocolate pudding.

DELICIOUS FUDGE SMOOTHIE

1 cup of whole milk
¼ cup of fudge sauce
1 tbsp chopped roasted almonds
2 scoops fudge chunk or toffee swirl ice cream

Add milk, almonds, and 2 scoops of ice cream into your blender and blend until smooth. Pour the smoothie into a chilled glass and drizzle the fudge sauce on top.

Peanut Split Smoothie

Chocomonster Smoothie

FROZEN MINT SMOOTHIE

8 fresh mint leaves
½ cup low-fat milk
2 scoops plain or vanilla frozen yogurt
sugar to taste
ice
mint leaves and whole raspberries to decorate

Combine mint leaves and low-fat milk in your blender and process until the mint leaves are finely chopped. Add frozen yogurt and sugar to taste. Serve over ice, garnished with raspberries.

BANANA & ORANGE CREAM SMOOTHIE

½ cup chilled orange juice
1 small banana, peeled and chopped
¼ cup half & half

½–1 tbsp whipped cream to decorate
orange slices to decorate

Pour orange juice then add banana and half & half into your blender and process until smooth. Pour the smoothie into a chilled glass and decorate with orange slices and whipped cream.

HAWAIIAN HEAVEN SMOOTHIE

2 cups milk
1 banana, frozen, broken into chunks
½ cup canned crushed pineapple, drained
2 tbsp sweetened shredded coconut
3 scoops vanilla yogurt
1 tbsp toasted chopped pecans, for topping (optional)

In a blender, combine milk, banana, pineapple, and coconut and blend until smooth. Add frozen yogurt and blend again.

PEAR & CINNAMON YOGURT SMOOTHIE

2 medium ripe pears, peeled, cored, and chopped
5¼ oz full-cream yogurt
¾ oz whipping cream
1½ tsp acacia honey
½ tsp powdered cinnamon
pinch of nutmeg
pinch of cinnamon sugar to decorate

Place the chopped pears into your blender along with the yogurt, cream, cinnamon, honey, and nutmeg. Process until silky smooth.

Pour into a glass, sprinkle with cinnamon sugar, and serve immediately.

BLUEBERRIES & CREAM SMOOTHIE

1 cup vanilla yogurt
1 cup crushed ice
½ cup frozen blueberries
1–2 cups whole milk
¼ cup sugar
½ tsp pure vanilla extract
heavy cream (optional, to decorate)

Put all the ingredients into a blender and blend until smooth. Pour into serving glasses and, if desired, drizzle a touch of heavy cream on top of each glass.

KEY LIME SMOOTHIE

1 container (6 oz) fat-free Key lime pie yogurt
1 ripe mango, sliced
2 cups 2% milk
1 cup spinach
juice and zest from 2 limes
¼ cup dates
½ tsp vanilla extract

Blend the mango with the yogurt and milk. Add the spinach and blend again. Finally, add the fruit and blend to the desired consistency.

Frozen Mint Smoothie

Hawaiian Heaven Smoothie

Pecan nuts

Key Lime Smoothie

MAPLE SYRUP SMOOTHIE

2 tbsp maple syrup
1 scoop vanilla ice cream
3–4 large ice cubes
whole milk or club soda

Place the maple syrup, ice cubes, and ice cream into your smoothie blender and process until smooth and frothy. Pour into chilled glasses and top off with club soda or milk.

GINGER & PEAR SMOOTHIE

1 ripe pear, cored and chopped
1¼ cups ginger ice cream
3 tbsp heavy whipping cream
2 ginger cookies, crumbled

Place the pear, ice cream, and heavy whipping cream into your blender and process for about 1 minute. Pour into glass and top with the crumbled cookies.

APPLE PIE SMOOTHIE

1 cup stewed apples
¼ tsp cinnamon
1 cup vanilla ice cream
3 tbsp whipped cream
1 oatmeal cookie, crumbled

Place all ingredients into your blender and mix for approximately one minute, or until smooth. Pour into glass and top smoothie with the cookie crumbles.

CHERRY SMOOTHIE

15 pitted black cherries, canned or fresh and very ripe
¾ cup cranberry juice
2 scoops vanilla frozen yogurt
¼ tsp almond extract
fresh cherries (optional, to decorate)

Place frozen yogurt, juice, cherries, and almond extract into your smoothie blender and process until silky smooth.
  Sift contents through a non-metallic strainer into an ice-filled glass. Decorate with fresh cherries.

PEACHES & DREAM

½ can peach halves; with juice
½ cup whole milk
¼ cup half & half
1½ scoops vanilla ice cream
3 tbsp peach liqueur
1 scoop peach ice cream
peach slices (optional, to decorate)

Place the peach halves with about ¼ cup juice into your smoothie blender and process until smooth. Pour about one-quarter of the puree into a jug and set aside. Add milk, half & half, ice cream, and the peach liqueur into your smoothie blender and process until smooth. Pour into a chilled glass and top with the remaining scoop of ice cream. Drizzle the reserved peach puree over the ice cream and decorate the glass with peach slices.

BAILEY'S LIQUEUR SMOOTHIE

1 cup vanilla ice cream
½ cup mascarpone
1 tbsp heavy whipping cream
1 tsp instant coffee dissolved in 1 tbsp boiling water
2 tbsp Bailey's liqueur
1 ladyfinger
cocoa powder (optional, to decorate)

Combine ice cream, mascarpone, and whipping cream in your smoothie blender and process for approximately one minute or until smooth. Pour into a glass. Mix the dissolved coffee and Bailey's liqueur and crumble the ladyfinger into the mixture. Stir the mixture into the glass. Dust the top of your smoothie with cocoa powder.

Cherry Smoothie

STRAWBERRY SMOOTHIE

1 cup strawberries, hulled
1 cup vanilla ce cream
½ cup ready-made custard
1 ladyfinger, crumbled
sugar sprinkles (optional, to decorate)

Place the ice cream, strawberries, and custard into your smoothie blender. Process for approximately 1 minute or until smooth. Pour into a glass and stir the crumbled ladyfinger through the mixture. Serve with the optional sugar sprinkles on top.

BANANA & TOFFEE SMOOTHIE

½ banana, peeled and chopped
½ cup whole milk
1 scoop toffee ice cream
½ tsp sugar (optional)
½ tsp lemon juice (optional)
grated chocolate and whipped cream to decorate

Place the banana, milk, ice cream, sugar, and lemon juice into your smoothie blender and process for about 30 seconds or until smooth. Pour into two glasses and serve with grated chocolate and whipping cream.

PEPPERMINT STICK SMOOTHIE

1 cup frozen vanilla yogurt
1 cup milk
at least 1 tbsp crushed peppermint candy
¾ cup ice

Combine yogurt, milk, peppermint candy, and ice. Peppermint bark and any other mint-based confections can be substituted for the crushed peppermint candy. Blend until smooth and creamy.

RASPBERRY & CHEESE SMOOTHIE

1 cup whole milk
2 tbsp cottage cheese
1–2 tbsp raspberry syrup
few drops of lime juice, or extra if needed
frozen raspberries for decoration

Place milk, cottage cheese, raspberry syrup, and lime juice into your smoothie blender and process until smooth. Taste, and add more lime juice if needed. Pour into a chilled glass and optionally decorate with 2 or 3 frozen raspberries.

MAGICAL STRAWBERRY SHAKE

½ can strawberries
¾ cup whole milk
¼ cup half & half
2 scoops vanilla or strawberry ice cream
ice cubes to serve

Drain the strawberries and place in your smoothie blender. Process until pureed. Add the milk, half & half, and ice cream then process again until smooth. Pour over ice cubes.

BLUEBERRY SMOOTHIE

2 cups milk
1 cup blueberries (fresh or frozen)
4 ounces cream cheese, cut into cubes
3 scoops vanilla frozen yogurt
2 tbsp graham cracker crumbs (optional, to decorate)

Combine milk, blueberries, and cream cheese in your blender and process until smooth. Add frozen yogurt and blend again. Top with graham-cracker crumbs.

Magical Strawberry Shake

AFTER-DINNER
COFFEE
SMOOTHIES

THOSE WHO WISH TO BYPASS A DESSERT SMOOTHIE CAN, NEVERTHELESS, ENJOY ANOTHER TRADITION: THE AFTER-DINNER COFFEE OR DECAF. ONLY THESE ARE MADE WITH ICE CREAM, FROZEN YOGURT, CHOCOLATE, AND OTHER INGREDIENTS NOT GENERALLY CONSIDERED PART OF A HEALTHY DIET—UNLESS YOU GO FOR THE GREEN COFFEE SMOOTHIE, WHICH INCLUDES SPINACH.

BASIC COFFEE SMOOTHIES

Option 1

1 cup strongly brewed coffee, cooled

1 cup milk, cold

2 heaping tsp instant vanilla pudding

1–3 tsp sugar

2 cups of small ice cubes (adding more will further thicken the smoothie)

Add all of the ingredients to the blender and blend until no ice chunks remain.

Optional extras

½ frozen banana, which will thicken the smoothie

2 tbsp chocolate syrup

dash of ground cinnamon

1 tsp instant coffee (for super coffee flavor)

¼ tsp almond extract

¼ tsp coconut extract

whipped cream on top

Option 2

1 cup ice

1 cup coffee

1 banana

1 cup milk or almond milk

1 tbsp honey

Blend in your blender until smooth and enjoy.

VANILLA COFFEE SMOOTHIE

1 cup French vanilla coffee, chilled

5 dates, pitted

1 tsp vanilla

¼ cup almonds, preferably raw

1 cup ice

Blend in your blender until smooth and enjoy.

COFFEE-SHOT PROTEIN SMOOTHIE

1 cup milk or almond milk

1 banana

1 tbsp peanut butter

1 tbsp cocoa powder

1 scoop chocolate protein powder

1 tbsp honey

1 cup coffee

1 cup ice

Blend in your blender until smooth and enjoy.

YOGURT COFFEE

¾ cup brewed coffee, chilled

¼ cup milk

¾ cup plain yogurt or vanilla yogurt

6–8 ice cubes

1½ tbsp sugar

Combine all ingredients in a blender jar and blend until smooth puree.

Optional variations

For a creamier smoothie, substitute ice cream for the milk.

For a mocha taste, add ½ tbsp sweet chocolate syrup and reduce the quantity of sugar to 1 tbsp.

FRAPPELICIOUS COFFEE SMOOTHIE

1 cup chilled coffee

½ cup milk or almond milk

½ tbsp coffee grounds

1 tbsp cocoa powder

1 tbsp chia seeds (optional, just to throw in some omega 3s)

Add ice to desired consistency.

Blend in your blender until smooth and enjoy.

Frappelicious Coffee Smoothie

GREEN DREAM COFFEE SMOOTHIE

3–4 tbsp coffee, chilled
1 cup milk or almond milk
1 banana
½ cup spinach
1 cup ice
1 tbsp honey
½ tbsp cocoa powder

Blend in your blender until smooth and enjoy. You won't be able to taste the spinach!

MOCHA JAVA COFFEE

½ cup brewed strong coffee (any variety), chilled
1 oz milk or dark chocolate (the richer, the better), coarsely chopped
1 cup coffee ice cream, slightly softened
1 cup milk
2 tbsp whipped cream
2 tsp milk or dark chocolate, grated

Blend coffee and chocolate in blender until chocolate is finely chopped. Add ice cream and milk; use pulsing action to blend until smooth.

FROZEN COFFEE CREAM

3 tbsp sugar-free whipped cream, divided
¼ cup brewed strong expresso, cooled
2 tbsp fat-free half-and-half
2 tsp low-cal sweetener
¼ tsp vanilla
1 cup ice cubes

Reserve 1 tbsp whipped cream; blend 2 tbsp whipped cream with all remaining ingredients except ice in blender until blended. Add ice; blend on high speed until thickened and smooth. Serve, topped with remaining whipped cream.

BANANA PROTEIN LATTE

1 scoop protein powder (whey or soy)
1 cup fat-free milk
¾ cup strong, black coffee (decaf is okay)
2 bananas, sliced
1 cup ice cubes

Blend ingredients together and enjoy this healthy pickup any time of the day.

TROPICANA COFFEE

½ cup cold fat-free milk
⅓ cup sugar-free French vanilla coffee
1 can (8 oz) crushed pineapple in juice, drained
1 small ripe banana
2 cups fat-free no-sugar-added vanilla ice cream, softened

Place all ingredients in blender container; cover. Blend on high speed until smooth.

DOUBLE-CHOC FRAPPACINO

⅓ cup semi-sweet, bittersweet, or milk chocolate chips, depending on your preference
1 cup milk (2% or whole for best taste)
3 tbsp chocolate or mocha syrup
dash of vanilla extract
2 tbsp granulated cane sugar
1½ cups ice

First, put the chocolate chips and ice in the blender, and blend for about 6 seconds. Add milk, chocolate syrup, vanilla extract, and cane sugar and blend until smooth.

Frozen Coffee Cream

INDEX – JUICES

INDEX – SMOOTHIES

ACKNOWLEDGMENTS

Special thanks to Jeremy Baile at RGB Digital for the creation of many of the special photographs in this book. www.rgbdigital.co.uk

Cover image: Shutterstock/Ingvar Bjork, main image: Shutterstock/Käfer photo • 1 Shutterstock/Ingvar Bjork • 2-3 Shutterstock/Tim UR • 4-7 Shutterstock/Gyuszko-Photo • 8-9 Shutterstock/verca • 10-11 Shutterstock/Tatiana Mihaliova • 12 Shutterstock/Petr Malyshev • 14-15 Shutterstock/Anna Hoychuk • 16-17 Shutterstock/Shebeko • 18t Shutterstock/Jiri Hera • 18b Shutterstock/Beat Bieler • 19 Shutterstock/Panom Pensawang • 20tl Shutterstock/djgis • 20br Shutterstock/nito • 21tl Shutterstock/Jon Le-Bon • 21tr (upper) Shutterstock/M. Unal Ozmen • 21tr (lower) Shutterstock/Shawn Hempel • 21c Shutterstock/M. Unal Ozmen • 21b Shutterstock/MaraZe • 22 Shutterstock/bestv • 23t Shutterstock/Enlightened Media • 23c Shutterstock/M. Unal Ozmen • 23b WikiMedia • 24 Shutterstock/Doczky • 26br Shutterstock/Wiktory • 26bl Shutterstock/Gregory Gerber • 27 Shutterstock/Mazzzur • 28t Shutterstock/Valentyn Volkov • 28b Shutterstock/Mazzzur • 29bl Shutterstock/Maksom Aan • 29r Shutterstock/joloei • 30bl Shutterstock/dafodilred • 30br Shutterstock/Lecic • 31 Shutterstock/Cristi Bastian • 32bl Shutterstock/Liljam • 32br Shutterstock/BMJ • 33bl Shutterstock/ElenaGaak • 33tr Shutterstock/Skreidzeleu • 34 Shutterstock/Lecic • 35 Shutterstock/Taiftin • 36bl Shutterstock/Gresei • 36br Shutterstock/Evoken • 37 Shutterstock/Anteromite • 38 Shutterstock/Candace Hartley • 39t Shutterstock/vanillaechoes • 39b Shutterstock/Maria Uspenkaya • 40 Shutterstock/B. and E. Dudzinscy • 41 Shutterstock/kukuruxa • 42bl Shutterstock/matka_Wariatka • 42br Shutterstock/janaph • 43bl Shutterstock/stockcreations • 43r Shutterstock/kungverylucky • 44bl Shutterstock/Tissiana Kelley • 45b Shutterstock/Christian Jung • 45t Shutterstock/vanillaechoes • 46t Shutterstock/Dream79 • 46b Shutterstock/Hannamariah • 47 Shutterstock/Valentyn Volkov • 48 Shutterstock/Africa Studio • 49 Shutterstock/Elena Eliseeva • 50b Shutterstock/Diana Taliun • 50t Shutterstock/Oxana Denezhkina • 51bl Shutterstock/Africa Studio • 51r Shutterstock/ETIENjones • 52b Shutterstock/Matee Nuserm • 52t Shutterstock/vanillaechoes • 53bl Shutterstock/Irina Schmidt • 53br Shutterstock/ Monika Gniot • 54bl Shutterstock/ER_09 • 54br Shutterstock/pilipphoto • 55b Shutterstock/Brandon Bourdages • 55t Shutterstock/Kati Molin • 56bl Shutterstock/verca • 56br Shutterstock/Denis and Yulia Pogostins • 57b Shutterstock/Africa Studio • 57t Shutterstock/Acambium64 • 58bl Shutterstock/Joel Vieira • 58br Shutterstock/Bahadir Yeniceri • 59 Shutterstock/azure • 60 Shutterstock/PhotoWeges • 61bl Shutterstock/Africa Studio • 61r Shutterstock/Ruud Morijn Photographer • 62b Shutterstock/Foodpictures • 62t Shutterstock/geniuscook_com • 63b Shutterstock/Anna Hoychuk • 63t Shutterstock/PhotoWeges • 64 Shutterstock/azure • 65b Shutterstock/Martin Lehmann • 65t Shutterstock/Janet Faye Hastings • 66b Shutterstock/scphoto60 • 66t Shutterstock/Nataliia Melnychuk • 67tr Shutterstock/Photographee.eu • 67br Shutterstock/Story • 68 Shutterstock/BMJ • 69bl Shutterstock/Sergey Goryachev • 69br Shutterstock/Norman Chan • 70bl Shutterstock/HandmadePictures • 70br Shutterstock/originalpunkt • 71b Shutterstock/Oleg Golovnev • 71t Shutterstock/anna_bobrowska • 72bl Shutterstock/Marilyn barbone • 72br Shutterstock/bonchan • 73bl Shutterstock/Brent Hofacker • 73br Shutterstock/Sandra Cunningham • 74 Shutterstock/Popov Nikolay • 76 Shutterstock/sematadesign • 77 Shutterstock/pick • 79tl Shutterstock/lauraslens • 79tr Shutterstock/MosayMay • 79bl Shutterstock/svry • 79br Shutterstock/Anna Hoychuk • 81 Shutterstock/Litt e_Desire • 83 Shutterstock/natahamam • 84 Shutterstock/Dream79 • 85 Shutterstock/Razmarinka • 86 Shutterstock/marekuliasz • 89 Shutterstock/van Ilaechoes • 90 Shutterstock/Matt Antonino • 91 Shutterstock/lola1960 • 92 Shutterstock/vanillaechoes • 93 Shutterstock/anshu18 • 94t Shutterstock/Olga Grygorashyk • 94b Shutterstock/liza1979 • 95 Shutterstock/Lesya Dolyuk • 96 Shutterstock/Melpomene • 97 Shutterstock/Anna Hoychuk • 98 Shutterstock/chuckstock • 99 Shutterstock/violeta pasat • 100 Shutterstock/Nicram Sabod • 102-105back Shutterstock/Ingvar Bjork • 102-103 Shutterstock/Africa Studio • 103tr Shutterstock/Anna Hoychuk • 103br Shutterstock/Elena Eliseeva • 104-105 Shutterstock/Anna Hoychuk • 105tl Shutterstock/Greg Nesbit Photography • 105tr Shutterstock/pearl7 • 106-125back Shutterstock/caesart • 107 RGB Digital Ltd • 109 RGB Digital Ltd • 110 RGB Digital Ltd • 111 RGB Digital Ltd • 112 Shutterstock/grafvision • 113 RGB Digital Ltd • 114 RGB Digital Ltd • 115 RGB Digital Ltd • 116 RGB Digital Ltd • 117 RGB Digital Ltd • 118 RGB Digital Ltd • 119 RGB Digital Ltd • 120 RGB Digital Ltd • 121 RGB Digital Ltd • 122 RGB Digital Ltd • 123 RGB Digital Ltd • 124 RGB Digital Ltd • 125 RGB Digital Ltd • 126 Shutterstock/Sunny Forest • 128-131back Shutterstock/Ingvar Bjork • 128-129 Shutterstock/Eve's Food Photography • 129tr Shutterstock/daughter • 129br Shutterstock/Kati Molin • 130-131 Shutterstock/lola1960 • 131tr Shutterstock/Melpomene • 131br Shutterstock/Sea Wave • 132-175back Shutterstock/Roxana Bashyrova • 133 Zach Copley (http://www.flickr.com/photos/22823034@N00/5969016977/in/photolist-a6sLMP-a6sPhv-a6vkBS) • 134 Shutterstock/Pefkos • 135 Shutterstock/Lukaszewicz • 136 Shutterstock/Piotr Wawrzyniuk • 137 Shutterstock/kviktor • 138 Shutterstock/Maxim Khytra • 139 Shutterstock/Olga Lyubkina • 140 Shutterstock/diamant24 • 141 Shutterstock/vanillaechoes • 142 Shutterstock/webwaffe • 143 Shutterstock/Svitlana-ua • 144 Shutterstock/Angela Andrews • 145 Shutterstock/Little_Desire • 146l Shutterstock/Aleksandra Kovac • 146r Shutterstock/Mariusz S. Jurgielewicz • 147 Shutterstock/elen_studio • 148 Shutterstock/Drozdowski • 149 Shutterstock/Maxim Khytra • 150 Shutterstock/S_Photo • 151 Shutterstock/kazoka • 152 Shutterstock/kazoka • 153 Shutterstock/Maxim Khytra • 154 RGB Digital Ltd • 155 RGB Digital Ltd • 156 Shutterstock/Steve Cukrov • 157 RGB Digital Ltd • 158 RGB Digital Ltd • 159 RGB Digital Ltd • 160 RGB Digital Ltd • 161 RGB Digital Ltd • 162 RGB Digital Ltd • 163 RGB Digital Ltd • 164 RGB Digital Ltd • 165 RGB Digital Ltd • 166 RGB Digital Ltd • 167 RGB Digital Ltd • 168 RGB Digital Ltd • 169 RGB Digital Ltd • 170 RGB Digital Ltd • 171 RGB Digital Ltd • 172 RGB Digital Ltd • 173 RGB Digital Ltd • 174 RGB Digital Ltd • 175 RGB Digital Ltd • 176 Shutterstock/danielo • 178-205back Shutterstock/Sundari • 178 RGB Digital Ltd • 179 RGB Digital Ltd • 180 RGB Digital Ltd • 181 RGB Digital Ltd • 182 RGB Digital Ltd • 183 RGB Digital Ltd • 184 Shutterstock/Lisovskaya Natalia • 185 RGB Digital Ltd • 186 RGB Digital Ltd • 187 RGB Digital Ltd • 188 RGB Digital Ltd • 189 RGB Digital Ltd • 190 RGB Digital Ltd • 191 RGB Digital Ltd • 192r RGB Digital Ltd •192r RGB Digital Ltd • 193 RGB Digital Ltd • 194 RGB Digital Ltd • 195 RGB Digital Ltd • 197 RGB Digital Ltd • 198 Shutterstock/enzodebernardo • 199 RGB Digital Ltd • 200 RGB Digital Ltd • 201 RGB Digital Ltd • 202 Shutterstock/bitt24 • 203 RGB Digital Ltd • 204t Shutterstock/Kesu • 204b Shutterstock/Saichon Phumma • 205 RGB Digital Ltd • 206 Shutterstock/Zeljko Radojko • 208-215back Shutterstock/Valentina Razumova • 208 Shutterstock/Gayvoronskaya_Yana • 209 RGB Digital Ltd • 210l RGB Digital Ltd • 210r RGB Digital Ltd • 211 Shutterstock/wanchai • 212 RGB Digital Ltd • 213 RGB Digital Ltd • 214 RGB Digital Ltd • 215 RGB Digital Ltd • 216 Shutterstock/Jure Porenta • 218-219back Shutterstock/Ingvar Bjork • 218-219 Shutterstock/pilipphoto • 219tr Shutterstock/Ildi Papp • 219br Shutterstock/Peredniankina • 220-243back Shutterstock/Ms.Moloko • 220 Shutterstock/Ana Blazic Pavlovic • 223t Shutterstock/IrinaFedotova • 223b Shutterstock/Wiktory • 225t Shutterstock/TZIDO SUN • 225bl Shutterstock/nanka •225br Shutterstock/Kenishirotie • 226 Shutterstock/Olga Lyubkina • 228 Shutterstock/ElenaGaak • 231 Shutterstock/svry • 233 Shutterstock/Ildi Papp • 235tl Shutterstock/Tobik • 235tr Shutterstock/Sergii Korshun • 235bl Shutterstock/ Igor Kovalchuk • 235br Shutterstock/kostrez • 236 Shutterstock/Pigdevil Photo • 239 Shutterstock/Liv friis-larsen • 240 Shutterstock/FOOKPHOTO.COM • 242 Shutterstock/isak55 • 243 Shutterstock/Little_Desire • 244 Shutterstock/Vorobyeva • 246-247back Shutterstock/Ingvar Bjork • 246-247 Shutterstock/Irina Schmidt • 247tr Shutterstock/ Shurrilina Maria • 247br Shutterstock/Africa Studio • 248-263back Shutterstock/Julia Ivantsova • 248 Shutterstock/Shebeko • 249 Shutterstock/stockcreations • 251 Shutterstock/vanillaechoes • 253 Shutterstock/Layland Masuda • 254 Shutterstock/Nitr • 255 Shutterstock/Francesco83 • 257 Shutterstock/HandmadePictures • 259 Shutterstock/Olyina • 261 Shutterstock/vanillaechoes • 263t Shutterstock/Anna-Mari West • 263b Shutterstock/DUSAN ZIDAR • 264 Shutterstock/Artem Samokhvalov • 266-267back Shutterstock/Ingvar Bjork • 266-267 Shutterstock/marekuliasz • 268-275back Shutterstock/amirage • 269 Shutterstock/Africa Studio • 271 Shutterstock/bitt24 • 273 Shutterstock/Nopphadon Jantranapaporn • 275 Shutterstock/HandmadePictures • 276 Shutterstock/Imageman • 278-293back Shutterstock/Curly Pat • 279 Shutterstock/sarsmis • 280t Shutterstock/Zigzag Mountain Art • 280c Shutterstock/mchin • 281 Shutterstock/Pinkcandy • 282 Shutterstock/Aleksandra Kovac • 283tl Shutterstock/ szefei • 283tr Shutterstock/Smit • 283bl Shutterstock/Ildi Papp • 283br Shutterstock/Stephanie Connell • 284 Shutterstock/clearimages • 285 Shutterstock/jreika • 286 Shutterstock/Apostolos Mastoris • 287 Shutterstock/NikDonetsk • 288 Shutterstock/Karen Wunderman and Shutterstock/S_Photo • 289 Shutterstock/Danie Nel • 290 Shutterstock/oksix • 291 Shutterstock/teleginatania • 292bl Shutterstock/margouillat photo • 292br Shutterstock/Lilyana Vynogradova • 293 Shutterstock/sarsmis • 294 Shutterstock/joannawnuk • 296-305back Shutterstock/alkkdsg • 297 Shutterstock/Brent Hofacker • 299t Shutterstock/MSPhotographic • 299b Shutterstock/Christopher Elwell • 301tl Shutterstock/Peredniankina 301tr Shutterstock/ Monika Olszewska • 301bl Shutterstock/nanka • 301br Shutterstock/Volosina • 303 Shutterstock/IngridHS • 305 Shutterstock/Kati Molin • 306 Shutterstock/Andrey Armyagov • 308-311back Shutterstock/Elinalee • 309 Shutterstock/hauhu • 311 Shutterstock/Palo_ok • 312-320 Shutterstock/Ingvar Bjork • 319 RGB Digital Ltd

Every effort has been made to trace all the copyright holders and we apologize in advance for any unintentional omissions. We would be pleased to insert the appropriate acknowledgment in any subsequent edition of this publication.